Simply Suppers

Easy Comfort Food Your Whole Family Will Love

by Jennifer Chandler

with photography by Natalie Root

THOMAS NELSON
Since 1798

NASHVILLE   DALLAS   MEXICO CITY   RIO DE JANEIRO

Published in Nashville, Tennessee, by Thomas Nelson. Thomas Nelson is a registered trademark of Thomas Nelson, Inc.

Photos by © Natalie Root Photography

Photos on pages xiv and 166 are from Photos.com.
Photos on pages 138 and 226 are from Brand X Pictures.

Thomas Nelson, Inc., titles may be purchased in bulk for educational, business, fund-raising, or sales promotional use. For information, please e-mail SpecialMarkets@ThomasNelson.com.

Library of Congress Control Number: 2010930935

ISBN: 978-1-4016-0059-4

Printed in the United States of America

10 11 12 13 14 QGT 6 5 4 3 2

To my favorite people to
enjoy supper with:
Paul, Hannah, and Sarah

Contents

Introduction

Comfort is a gift we give our friends and family when we feed them.

Good food isn't about being gourmet . . . it's about being delicious. In fact, some of our favorite foods are the simplest dishes.

Think about it. Aren't there certain foods that make you feel good inside just thinking about them?

Maybe a gooey mac'n'cheese, a perfectly roasted chicken, or creamy mashed potatoes? For me, it's warm brownies fresh from the oven, a simple grilled cheese sandwich, and my grandmother's eggplant casserole.

Comfort food is all about home cooking. Dishes that warm our souls and put a smile on our faces. That's what I want for supper. Don't you?

I wrote *Simply Suppers* to help you put good food on your table. This book includes my tried-and-true recipes that I make over and over again. My wish is that some of the recipes in this book will become your favorites too.

Some of the recipes will be familiar. Some dishes may evoke memories of your childhood. Some may be new to you. But I guarantee they will all taste great. These are the kinds of recipes that you will want to share at supper clubs, pass down through generations of your family, and swap over coffee.

Many of these dishes can be thrown together in minutes; others need to simmer slowly. But all are simple to prepare.

The recipes in *Simply Suppers* are those of family traditions. So start cooking together. Include your family, friends, and children in the kitchen. And no matter how simple the meal, sit down together, and enjoy the comfort of good food and good company.

Enjoy!

What's for Supper?

I t's a daily question. Whether eating alone or feeding others, you will ask yourself (or be asked) "What's for supper?"

With time at a premium, many of us opt for processed convenience foods or on-the-go meals from fast-food restaurants for dinner. Not only are these choices usually more expensive than home-made, they are often not the healthiest or tastiest.

Simply Suppers gives you an alternative.

It is simple to pull together delicious home-cooked meals if you are equipped with a few strategies.

- Be armed with a repertoire of basic cooking techniques. When choosing the recipes to include in this book, I intentionally included a variety of cooking skills. Sautéing, pan-roasting, braising, baking, and making sauces are all simple techniques that can be used to make an infinite number of dishes.
- Make it easy on yourself and take the stress out of cooking. Use shortcut ingredients, like rotisserie chicken and frozen vegetables. Do whatever you can in advance, keeping in mind that some dishes actually taste better the next day. Make double batches of recipes that freeze well so you will always have a home-cooked meal available in the freezer.
- Use the best ingredients. The key to delicious food is simple: use fresh, in-season, top-quality ingredients. And remember, best does not always mean the most expensive. Let flavor be your guide when choosing what goes into your food.
- Maintain a well-stocked kitchen (see page xii for my Well-Stocked Kitchen list). Having the right ingredients in your pantry, refrigerator, and freezer can make the difference between ordering take-out pizza and having a delicious last-minute meal.
- Taste as you go. By tasting a spoonful here and there through the cooking process, you will

see if you need to add a little more of something. And always be sure to taste your dish before serving to make sure you don't need one more dash of salt or pepper or a tablespoon of cream or butter to round out the flavor.

Tips

What are the questions you often have when reading a recipe?

What can I do ahead? Can I freeze this? What is a good substitute?

I tried to think of all the different tips and variations that I wished the cookbooks on my shelves offered. Here are six basic tips you will find throughout *Simply Suppers* that will help you get healthy, delicious meals on the table . . . even on your busiest day.

Cooking Tips: Detailed information on cooking techniques, substitutes, and "Food Facts" about the dishes and specific ingredients.

Variations: Tips on how to put a unique spin on a classic dish.

Do Ahead: Tips and strategies to take the stress out of dinnertime.

Time-Saving Tips: Substitutes and shortcuts to save a little time in the kitchen.

Back-to-the-Basics: Recipe modifications for a simpler version.

Freezes Well: This icon lets you know which dishes are perfect for freezing.

30 in about 30

30 recipes that can quickly be whipped up in about 30 minutes

10 Leftover Chicken Makeovers

Here are 10 recipes to turn your leftovers (or a rotisserie chicken from your local market) into something delicious.

1. White Bean Chicken Chili (page 21)
2. Chicken Tortilla Soup (page 7)
3. Corn Chowder (page 3)
4. Chicken à la King (page 29)
5. Chicken Pot Pie (page 38)
6. Chicken Enchiladas with Salsa Verde (page 35)
7. Shrimp, Chicken, and Sausage Jambalaya (page 91)
8. Chicken Tetrazzini (page 100)
9. Chicken, Roasted Poblano, and Corn Quesadillas (page 121)
10. Chicken, Caramelized Onion, and Apple Pizza (page 119)

20 Freezer Go-To's

When making these recipes, make a double batch to freeze. This way you'll always have a home-cooked meal, even if you don't have time to cook.

1. Vegetable Beef Soup (page 19)
2. Pa's Chicken Noodle Soup (page 5)
3. White Bean Chicken Chili (page 21)
4. Chili Con Carne (page 9)
5. Creamy Tomato Soup (page 11)
6. Chicken Tortilla Soup (page 7)
7. French Onion Soup (page 13)
8. Lentil and Sausage Soup (page 15)
9. Chicken à la King (page 29)
10. Chicken Pot Pie (page 38)
11. Turkey Burgers (page 47)
12. Potato Chip Chicken Fingers (page 43)
13. Slow Cooker Beef Stew (page 63)
14. Italian Meatloaf (page 66)
15. Carnitas Pork Tacos (page 59)
16. Chicken Tetrazzini (page 100)
17. Mama's Spaghetti (page 111)
18. Vongole Clam Sauce (page 115)
19. Italian Sausage and Spinach Lasagna (page 106)
20. Sloppy Joes (page 135)

A Well-Stocked Kitchen

Keeping a well-stocked kitchen will make meal preparation a breeze.

If you have this basic list of kitchen utensils and ingredients on hand, making the recipes in this book will be effortless. And there will always be something to eat . . . no matter what time of day it is or who stops by for supper.

Basic Kitchen Utensils

Set of graduated, straight-edge measuring cups made for dry ingredients
10-inch cast-iron skillet, well-seasoned
Set of measuring spoons
12-inch ovenproof sauté pan
Glass liquid measuring cup
8-quart stockpot
Small whisk
2-quart saucepan with lid
Tongs
Baking dishes (one 8- x 8-inch and one 9- x 13-inch)
Flat metal spatula
9-inch pie dish
Heatproof rubber spatula
Large, rimmed baking sheet

Vegetable peeler (the rubber-handled ones are easier on your hands)
Colander
Can opener
Traditional four-sided cheese grater
Peppermill
Blender or food processor
Mixing bowls (both large and small)
Aluminum foil and plastic wrap
Good, sharp knives (a small paring knife and a 6- to 8-inch chef knife are a must)
Resealable containers and baggies (several sizes for leftovers)
Cutting boards (at least two—one for raw meats and another for everything else)

Not Essential but Fun to Have

Garlic press
Fine sieve
Metal fish spatula
Removable-bottom tart pans
Microplane zesters (both fine and coarse)

7-quart Dutch oven (I love the enameled cast-iron ones.)
Soup ladle
Stand mixer
Lemon juicer
Immersion blender

Pantry Items

Kosher salt

Rice

Black peppercorns for your peppermill

Pastas

Olive oil

Spices (thyme, oregano, and basil)

Vegetable or canola oil

Pure vanilla extract

Mustards (whole-grain, Dijon, and yellow)

All-purpose flour

Bread crumbs

Granulated sugar

Canned tomatoes (whole, diced, and pureed)

Light and dark brown sugars

Perishable/Refrigerator Items

Chicken stock

Yellow onions

Unsalted butter

Celery

Mayonnaise

Carrots

Milk

Lemons

Heavy cream

Green bell peppers

Cheeses (Parmesan, cheddar, and Gruyère)

Fresh herbs (basil, cilantro, or flat-leaf parsley)

Eggs

Potatoes

Garlic

Freezer Items

Ground beef

Unbaked pie crust

Italian sausage

Tortillas

Shrimp

Bread

Frozen Vegetables (peas, green beans, corn, spinach)

Nuts (pine nuts, walnuts, almonds, pecans)

SOUPS

Corn Chowder

Cold, dreary weather doesn't stand a chance with a bowl of this creamy, hearty corn chowder. Fresh corn is always ideal, but in the dead of winter, frozen corn is the perfect substitute.

2	tablespoons unsalted butter		2	cups half-and-half
1	tablespoon olive oil		4	cups corn kernels (about 2 pounds frozen or 8 ears fresh)
1	cup finely diced yellow onion (1 large onion)			Kosher salt and freshly ground black pepper
2	garlic cloves, minced		1/2	cup shredded cheddar cheese (optional)
1/2	teaspoon dried thyme		1/4	cup crumbled cooked bacon (optional)
1/4	cup all-purpose flour			
6	cups chicken stock			
4	cups peeled and diced white boiling potatoes (about 1 1/2 pounds or 4 large potatoes)			

▶ In a large stockpot over medium-high heat, warm the butter and oil until a few droplets of water sizzle when carefully sprinkled in the pot. Add the onion, garlic, and thyme and cook, stirring occasionally, until soft, about 4 minutes. Dust the onion mixture with the flour and stir to coat. Cook for 2 minutes. Whisk in the chicken stock and over high heat, bring the mixture to a boil. Add the potatoes and bring the mixture back to a boil. Stir in the half-and-half.

Reduce the heat to medium and simmer uncovered for 15 minutes, or until the potatoes are tender.

▶ Add the corn and simmer until the corn is soft, about 15 minutes. Season with salt and pepper to taste. Serve hot, garnished with cheddar cheese and bacon, if desired.

Serves 8.

 Variations: Add a cup of diced or shredded cooked chicken to make this already-satisfying soup even heartier.

For a "Southwestern" kick, stir in a can (4.5-ounce) of diced green chilies with the onions, and garnish the finished soup with tortilla chips.

Pa's Chicken Noodle Soup

While most chicken noodle soups are accredited to grandmas, this recipe belongs to my dad (affectionately known as "Pa" by my girls). It not only cures all, but it is so good you'll want a bowl even when you are well!

2   split bone-in, skin-on chicken breasts
     (about 1³/4 pounds)
Kosher salt and freshly ground black pepper
1   tablespoon olive oil
1/2 cup finely diced yellow onion (1 small onion)
1/2 cup thinly sliced celery (about 2 ribs)
1/2 cup finely diced carrots (about 2 carrots)

1   bay leaf
1   teaspoon finely chopped fresh rosemary
     leaves
8   cups chicken stock
4   cups egg noodles, cooked per the package
     directions

▶ Rinse the chicken and pat dry with paper towels. Generously season the chicken with salt and pepper. In a large stockpot over medium-high heat, warm the oil until a few droplets of water sizzle when carefully sprinkled in the pot. Add the chicken and sear until golden brown on both sides, about 6 minutes. Transfer the chicken to a plate.

▶ Drain all but about 1 tablespoon of fat from the pot. Add the onion, celery, carrots, bay leaf, and rosemary. Sauté, stirring often, until soft, about 10 minutes. Add the stock and return the chicken to the pot. Over high heat, bring the stock to a boil. Reduce the heat to medium-low and simmer until the chicken is tender

and cooked through, about 45 minutes. Using a slotted spoon, transfer the cooked chicken to a large bowl to cool. Keep the broth warm in the pot. Once the chicken is cool enough to handle, remove the meat from the bones and discard the skin. Shred the chicken meat into 2-inch pieces.

▶ Season the broth with salt and pepper to taste. Discard the bay leaf. Return the chicken to the pot and reheat the soup until the chicken is warmed through. Place the cooked egg noodles in the serving bowl and ladle the hot soup over the top.

Serves 6.

 Variation: This soup is also delicious ladled over rice instead of the noodles.

 Freezes Well: If possible, it is best to freeze the soup without the noodles because the noodles will absorb the broth and become mushy. When the soup is thawed, simply add freshly cooked noodles.

Chicken Tortilla Soup

Whenever I have a cooking question, the first person I turn to is my friend Melissa Petersen. This recipe is so easy you won't believe that it came from such a talented cook.

Vegetable oil, for frying the tortillas
4 small (4-inch) corn tortillas, cut into 1/4-inch strips
Kosher salt and freshly ground black pepper
1 tablespoon olive oil
1/2 cup finely diced yellow onion (1 small onion)
1 clove garlic, minced
1/4 teaspoon ground cumin

1/2 teaspoon dried oregano
1 can (28-ounce) diced tomatoes with juice
3 cups chicken stock
2 cups shredded cooked chicken
3/4 cup shredded Monterey Jack cheese
1 avocado, peeled, seeded, and cut in 1/2-inch cubes
1/4 cup finely chopped fresh cilantro leaves

▸ To prepare the tortilla strips, pour enough oil into a large stockpot so that you have a quarter-inch layer of oil. Warm the oil on medium-high heat until a few droplets of water sizzle when carefully sprinkled in the pot or a thermometer reads 375 degrees. In batches, fry the tortilla strips until golden brown on both sides, about 30 seconds to 1 minute per side. Use metal tongs or a slotted spoon to lift the tortilla strips out of the pan, draining the excess oil as you do so. (The tortilla strips should be fairly stiff and crisp. If not, the oil is not hot enough.) Transfer the tortilla strips to a paper towel–lined plate to absorb the excess oil. Lightly season with salt and pepper while they are still warm.

▸ In another large stockpot over medium-high heat, warm the olive oil until a few droplets of water sizzle when carefully sprinkled in the pot. Add the onion and sauté until soft, about 5 minutes. Add the garlic, cumin, and oregano, and cook until fragrant, about 1 minute. Add the tomatoes, chicken stock, and shredded chicken. Over high heat, bring the mixture to a boil. Reduce the heat to medium and simmer until the flavors have melded, about 15 minutes. Season with salt and pepper to taste.

▸ Ladle the soup into bowls and garnish with the fried tortilla strips, cheese, avocado, and fresh cilantro. Serve immediately.

Serves 4.

 Cooking Tip: If you want a little extra kick, add a few dashes of your favorite hot sauce.

 Time-Saving Tip: I like the shape and taste of homemade tortilla strips. They only take about 5 minutes to make. But if you are short on time, just pick up a bag of tortilla chips and use those instead.

 Do Ahead: The soup can be made the night before or frozen in advance. Just be sure to add the garnishes (tortilla strips, cheese, and avocado) just before serving.

Chili con Carne

This Southwestern favorite is ideal for a dinner party. Simply set out colorful bowls and encourage guests to serve themselves straight from the pot. Your guests will have a ball concocting their own signature dish with toppings such as sour cream, fresh cilantro, jalapeños, minced onion, shredded cheese, diced mild green chilies, and hot sauce.

1	tablespoon vegetable oil
1 1/2	pounds ground beef
1/2	cup finely diced yellow onion (1 small onion)
1/2	cup seeded and finely diced green bell pepper (1 small pepper)
4	cloves garlic, minced
2	tablespoons chili powder
2	teaspoons ground cumin
1	teaspoon dried oregano

1/4	teaspoon cayenne pepper
1	dash paprika
1	bay leaf
1	can (14.5-ounce) whole tomatoes with juice
3	tablespoons tomato paste
1	teaspoon granulated sugar
2	cups water

Kosher salt and freshly ground black pepper

▶ In a large stockpot over medium-high heat, warm the oil until a few droplets of water sizzle when carefully sprinkled in the pot. Add the meat and cook, stirring occasionally, until browned and cooked through, about 5 minutes. Add the onion, green bell pepper, garlic, chili powder, cumin, oregano, cayenne, paprika, and bay leaf. Cook, stirring, until the vegetables are soft, about 4 minutes.

▶ Add the whole tomatoes, breaking them up with a spoon or fork. Add the tomato paste, sugar, and water. Stir well to combine. Season with salt and pepper to taste. Over high heat, bring the mixture to a boil. Reduce the heat to medium-low and simmer uncovered, stirring occasionally, until thickened, about 30 minutes. Adjust seasonings as necessary. Discard the bay leaf. Serve hot.

Serves 6.

 Cooking Tip: If you like beans in your chili, add a drained can (15-ounce) of red kidney beans while the chili is simmering.

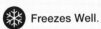 **Freezes Well**.

Creamy Tomato Soup

A steamy bowl of creamy tomato soup and a warm grilled cheese sandwich is a marriage made in heaven.

2   tablespoons olive oil
1/2   cup finely diced yellow onion (1 small onion)
4   cloves garlic, minced
1/4   teaspoon crushed red pepper flakes
2   cans (28-ounce) whole tomatoes with juice
2   teaspoons dried oregano

1/2   teaspoon dried thyme
1   tablespoon granulated sugar
4   cups chicken stock
1/2   cup heavy cream
Kosher salt and freshly ground black pepper

▸ In a large stockpot over medium-high heat, warm the oil until a few droplets of water sizzle when carefully sprinkled in the pot. Add the onion, garlic, and red pepper flakes, and cook, stirring, until the onions are soft, about 5 minutes.

▸ Add the whole tomatoes, breaking them up with a spoon or fork. Add the oregano, thyme, and sugar, and stir to combine. Pour in the chicken stock and stir to combine. Over high heat, bring the mixture to a boil.

Lower the heat to medium-low and simmer, uncovered, until the tomatoes have softened and the soup has thickened, about 30 minutes.

▸ Using an immersion blender, carefully puree the soup until smooth. Whisk in the heavy cream and season with salt and pepper to taste. Serve hot.

Serves 4 to 6.

 Cooking Tips: If you don't have an immersion blender, you can easily puree this soup in a countertop blender. Whenever pureeing hot liquid in a blender, remove the heat cap in the lid and cover with a towel to prevent the mixture from exploding all over you and your kitchen. Work in batches, only filling the blender half full. Also be sure to hold the lid down tightly while pureeing.

The granulated sugar in this recipe helps balance the acidity of the canned tomatoes.

French Onion Soup

Despite its fancy presentation, French onion soup is surprisingly easy to make. Caramelizing the onions and topping the soup with a delicious, nutty cheese is the secret to this classic French bistro soup.

1/2	cup unsalted butter
6	cups thinly sliced yellow onions (about 4 large onions)
2	cloves garlic, minced
2	bay leaves
2	sprigs fresh thyme
2	tablespoons cognac

1	cup dry white wine
3	tablespoons all-purpose flour
8	cups beef stock

Kosher salt and freshly ground black pepper

1	baguette, thinly sliced into at least 8 rounds

1 1/2 cups grated Gruyère cheese

▸ In a large stockpot or Dutch oven over medium heat, melt the butter. Add the onion, garlic, bay leaves, and thyme, and cook, stirring often, until soft and caramel colored, about 20 to 30 minutes.

▸ Add the cognac and cook until the liquid has almost evaporated, about 2 minutes. Add the white wine and simmer uncovered until the wine has almost evaporated, about 8 minutes. Dust the onion mixture with the flour and stir to coat. Cook until thickened, about 2 minutes.

▸ Pour in the beef stock and, over high heat, bring the mixture to a boil. Lower the temperature to medium and simmer, uncovered, until the flavors have melded, about 15 minutes. Season with salt and pepper to taste. Discard the bay leaves and thyme sprigs.

▸ Preheat the broiler. Toast the bread lightly. Ladle the soup into ovenproof bowls. Top each bowl with 2 slices of the toasted bread and 1/4 cup of cheese. Broil until the cheese is melted, about 3 to 5 minutes. Serve hot.

Serves 6.

Cooking Tip: If you do not have ovenproof bowls, no worries. Arrange the baguette slices on a baking sheet in a single layer, sprinkle the slices with the cheese, and broil until bubbly and golden brown, about 3 to 5 minutes. Top the soup with the cheesy baguette slices.

Freezes Well: French onion soup freezes well without the cheesy toast topping. When ready to eat, top the thawed and reheated soup with the baguette slices and cheese.

Lentil and Sausage Soup

This hearty soup is a favorite at my friend Patricia Vieira Wilson's house. She serves it with crusty bread and a green salad.

2	tablespoons olive oil
1/2	cup finely diced country ham
1	cup finely diced yellow onion (1 large onion)
3	cloves garlic, minced
1	cup thinly sliced celery (about 3 to 4 ribs)
1 1/2	cups finely diced carrots (about 5 carrots)
2	bay leaves
1	tablespoon dried thyme

6	cups chicken stock
4	cups water, divided
1	package (16-ounce) dried lentils, rinsed and sorted
	Kosher salt and freshly ground black pepper
1	pound smoked Andouille sausage, thinly sliced into rounds

▶ In a large stockpot over medium-high heat, warm the oil until a few droplets of water sizzle when carefully sprinkled in the pot. Add the country ham and sauté until lightly browned, about 3 minutes. Add the onion and garlic and sauté until soft, about 6 minutes. Add the celery and carrots and sauté another 2 to 3 minutes. Add the bay leaves, thyme, chicken stock, 2 cups of the water, and lentils, and stir to combine. Over high heat, bring to a boil. Reduce the heat to medium-low and simmer, covered, stirring occasionally, until lentils are al dente, about 45 minutes. Season with salt and pepper to taste.

▶ Add the sausage and remaining 2 cups of water and cook until the lentils are tender and the soup has thickened, about 20 minutes. Discard the bay leaves. Adjust seasonings as needed. Serve hot.

Serves 6.

 Variations: Andouille is my favorite smoked sausage, and I just love the spicy kick it gives to this dish. If you have another favorite smoked sausage, feel free to substitute it for the Andouille. Turkey sausage is a heart-healthy alternative.

Omit the ham and sausage and substitute vegetable stock for a flavorful vegetarian version of this hearty soup.

 Cooking Tip: If you can't find country ham at your local market, thick-cut prosciutto and bacon are acceptable substitutes.

 Freezes Well.

Mashed Potato Soup

Ever wonder what to do with those leftover mashed potatoes? Here's a delicious solution.

4   tablespoons unsalted butter
1/4 cup finely diced yellow onion
     (1/2 small onion)
4   tablespoons all-purpose flour
3   cups chicken stock
2¹/2 cups leftover mashed potatoes

1   cup heavy cream
Kosher salt and freshly ground black pepper
1/4 cup crumbled cooked bacon (optional)
1   small tomato, diced (optional)
2   tablespoons thinly sliced scallions (optional)

▶ In a large stockpot over medium-high heat, melt the butter. Add the onion and cook until soft, about 3 minutes. Dust the onions with the flour and cook, stirring, until lightly golden, about 1 minute. Whisk in the chicken stock. Over high heat, bring the mixture to a boil. Cook until slightly thickened, about 2 to 3 minutes. Reduce the heat to medium and whisk in the mashed potatoes until you have a smooth consistency.

Gradually whisk in the heavy cream. Season with salt and pepper to taste. Cook until the mixture is heated through, about 4 to 5 minutes. Serve hot, garnished with crumbled bacon, diced tomatoes, and scallions, if desired.

Serves 4.

 Cooking Tips: If you don't have mashed potatoes handy, you can still make this soup. Just peel and dice 1¹/2 pounds of red potatoes. Place the raw potatoes and a pinch of salt in a pot of cold water. Over high heat, bring to a boil. Reduce the heat to medium and simmer until the potatoes are fork tender. Drain the potatoes and mash them.

If the soup is too thick, you can thin it by adding a little more chicken stock.

 Variation: For a vegetarian version, substitute vegetable stock for the chicken stock and omit the bacon.

 Time-Saving Tip: You can pick up some premade mashed potatoes at your local market if you don't have leftovers or time to mash a fresh batch.

Vegetable Beef Soup

I always have several containers of this soup in my freezer. It is my healthy "go-to" meal when I don't have time to cook.

1	pound beef chuck roast or stew meat, trimmed and cut into 1-inch cubes
	Kosher salt and freshly ground black pepper
2	tablespoons olive oil
1/2	cup finely diced yellow onion (1 small onion)
1	can (28-ounce) diced tomatoes with juice
1	teaspoon dried basil
1	teaspoon dried thyme

1	teaspoon dried oregano
1	cup frozen peas
1	cup frozen cut green beans
1	cup frozen corn kernels
1	cup frozen lima beans
1	cup peeled and diced carrots
6	cups chicken stock

▸ Pat the meat dry with a paper towel and generously season with salt and pepper. In a large stockpot over medium-high heat, warm the oil until a few droplets of water sizzle when carefully sprinkled in the pot. Add the meat and cook, stirring occasionally, until browned on all sides, about 8 minutes. Transfer the meat to a plate and reserve. Drain all but about 1 tablespoon of fat from the pot.

▸ Reduce the heat to medium. Add the onions and cook, stirring occasionally, until soft, about 4 minutes.

Add the tomatoes, basil, thyme, and oregano. Season with salt and pepper to taste. Add the reserved meat, peas, green beans, corn, lima beans, carrots, and chicken stock. Stir to combine. Over high heat, bring the soup to a boil. Reduce the heat to medium-low and simmer, covered, until the flavors have melded, about 45 minutes. Adjust the seasonings as needed. Serve hot.

Serves 6.

 Cooking Tip: You can always use fresh vegetables if you prefer, but I just love the ease of using frozen vegetables.

Some products in the frozen food section may even be healthier than the fresh variety. Several research studies show that freezing vegetables and fruits "locks in" important vitamins and stops the nutrient loss that can occur in fresh vegetables that are often picked weeks before they make it to the grocery store aisles.

 Time-Saving Tip: No need to thaw the frozen vegetables. They will thaw as they cook.

 Freezes Well.

White Bean Chicken Chili

This hearty soup was a favorite at my restaurant, Cheffie's Market and More. Serve it on its own, or garnish this tasty chili with your favorite Tex-Mex toppings.

1	tablespoon olive oil
1/2	cup finely diced yellow onion (1 small onion)
1/3	cup seeded and finely diced poblano pepper (1/2 pepper)
1	can (4.5-ounce) diced green chilies
4	cups chicken stock
2	cups shredded cooked chicken
4	cans (15-ounce) cannellini beans

1	tablespoon dried thyme
1/2	teaspoon ground cumin
	Kosher salt and freshly ground black pepper
6	tablespoons sour cream (optional)
1/4	cup sliced fresh or pickled jalapeños (optional)
1/4	cup fresh cilantro leaves (optional)

▶ In a large stockpot over medium-high heat, warm the oil until a few droplets of water sizzle when carefully sprinkled in the pot. Add the onion and poblano pepper, and sauté until soft, about 10 minutes. Add the green chilies and sauté until combined, about 1 minute.

▶ Add the chicken stock, chicken, beans, thyme, and cumin. Season with salt and pepper to taste. Over high heat, bring to a boil. Reduce the heat to medium-low and simmer uncovered, stirring occasionally, until thickened, about 35 to 40 minutes. Adjust seasonings as needed.

▶ Serve hot. Garnish with a dollop of sour cream, sliced jalapeños, and fresh cilantro, if desired.

Serves 6.

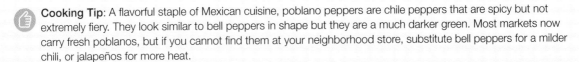

Cooking Tip: A flavorful staple of Mexican cuisine, poblano peppers are chile peppers that are spicy but not extremely fiery. They look similar to bell peppers in shape but they are a much darker green. Most markets now carry fresh poblanos, but if you cannot find them at your neighborhood store, substitute bell peppers for a milder chili, or jalapeños for more heat.

Time-Saving Tip: Short on time? Pick up a rotisserie chicken at your local grocery store for this recipe.

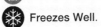

❄ **Freezes Well**.

POULTRY

Opposite page: Chicken Pot Pie (page 38)

Arroz con Pollo

"It's like a piñata! Just a big party in your mouth!" joked my good friend Lucia Heros as she served me a bowl of her Latin-inspired rice and chicken dish. And you know what? With all these colors and flavors together in one pot . . . I agree. It's downright "delicioso"!

4 split, bone-in, skin-on chicken breasts (about 3 pounds)
Kosher salt and freshly ground black pepper
1 tablespoon olive oil
1 tablespoon unsalted butter
1/2 cup finely diced yellow onion (1 small onion)
1/2 cup seeded and finely diced green bell pepper (1 small pepper)

1/2 cup seeded and finely diced red bell pepper (1 small pepper)
1 package (10-ounce) uncooked saffron yellow rice
1 can (28-ounce) diced tomatoes with juice
2 1/2 cups chicken stock
2 cups frozen mixed vegetables (carrots, corn, peas, lima beans, and green beans)
2 tablespoons apple cider vinegar

▶ Using a large sharp, knife or kitchen shears, cut each chicken breast into three equal-size pieces. Rinse the chicken and pat dry with paper towels. Generously season the chicken with salt and pepper. In a large stockpot or Dutch oven over medium-high heat, warm the oil and butter until a few droplets of water sizzle when carefully sprinkled in the pot. Cook the chicken, turning occasionally, until nicely browned on all sides, about 5 minutes. Transfer the chicken to a plate and reserve.

▶ Drain all but about 1 tablespoon of fat from the pot. Add the onions, green bell pepper, and red bell pepper. Cook, stirring occasionally, until soft, about 10 minutes. Add the rice and cook, stirring occasionally, until the rice is translucent, about 3 minutes. Add the diced tomatoes, chicken stock, frozen vegetables, and vinegar. Season with salt and pepper to taste. Return the chicken to the pot and stir to combine.

▶ Over high heat, bring the mixture to a boil. Reduce the heat to medium-low, cover, and simmer until the rice is tender and most of the liquid has been absorbed, about 50 to 60 minutes. Adjust seasonings as needed. Serve hot.

Serves 6 to 8.

 Cooking Tip: Saffron yellow rice is white rice that has been flavored (and colored) with the exotic spice saffron. Look for it at your local market in the rice section. Using yellow rice in this dish adds both flavor and color.

 Time-Saving Tip: No need to thaw the frozen vegetables. They will thaw as they cook.

Barbecue Chicken Drumsticks

When short on time, baked chicken is the way to go. I like to slather mine in barbecue sauce. Always add the sauce toward the end of the cooking time so it doesn't burn.

12 chicken drumsticks (about 3 pounds)
2 tablespoons olive oil

Kosher salt and freshly ground black pepper
1 cup barbecue sauce, divided

▸ Preheat the oven to 395 degrees.

▸ Rinse the chicken and pat dry with paper towels. Place the chicken in a roasting pan and lightly coat with the olive oil. Generously season the chicken with salt and pepper. Bake until golden, about 25 minutes.

▸ Remove the baking dish from the oven and spoon 1/2 cup of the barbecue sauce over the chicken. Toss to coat. Return the baking dish to the oven and bake until the chicken is cooked through and the sauce is caramelized, about 15 minutes.

▸ In a small saucepan or microwave, warm the remaining 1/2 cup of sauce. Pour the warm sauce over the cooked chicken. Serve warm.

Serves 4.

 Cooking Tip: Want a little extra kick? My friend Chef Kevin Roberts, spokesperson for Frank's® RedHot® and a fellow cookbook author, prefers to spice it up with hot sauce. He uses equal parts hot sauce and barbecue sauce for a spicy concoction. You can adjust the proportions based on how much heat your taste buds prefer.

Chicken á la King

One of my favorite meals as a kid was chicken á la king out of the can, slathered over toasted white bread. Here is a flavorful homemade version to satisfy your more grown-up taste buds.

4	tablespoons unsalted butter
1	cup thinly sliced button mushrooms
1/4	cup finely diced yellow onion (1/2 small onion)
1/4	cup seeded and finely diced green bell pepper (1/2 small pepper)
1	clove garlic, minced
1/4	cup all-purpose flour
2	tablespoons sherry

1 1/2	cups half-and-half
1	cup chicken stock
	Kosher salt and freshly ground pepper
2	cups shredded or diced cooked chicken
1/4	cup finely diced roasted red bell pepper
1	tablespoon finely chopped fresh flat-leaf parsley
4	thick slices white sandwich bread, lightly toasted

▶ In a large saucepan over medium heat, melt the butter. Add the mushrooms, onions, bell pepper, and garlic, and cook until the vegetables are soft, about 5 minutes. Dust the vegetables with the flour and stir to coat everything well. Cook until golden, about 2 minutes. Add the sherry and cook until the liquid has almost evaporated, about 1 minute. Stir in the half-and-half and chicken stock. Over high heat, bring the mixture back to a boil. Reduce the heat to medium-low and simmer, stirring occasionally, until the sauce thickens, about 5 minutes. Season with salt and pepper to taste. Add the chicken, red bell pepper, and parsley, and stir to combine. Cook until the chicken is warmed through, about 3 to 4 minutes.

▶ To serve, arrange a slice of toast on each plate. Spoon the sauce over the toast. Serve immediately.

Serves 4.

Cooking Tip: I don't always have half-and-half in my fridge. You can easily make your own by mixing equal parts of milk and heavy cream. Using just milk will result in a lighter sauce, and conversely, using just heavy cream will give you a richer sauce.

Back-to-the-Basics: I like the sophisticated flavor that sherry lends to this dish, but the results will still be delicious if you prefer to omit it.

Chicken and Dumplings

A rich, flavorful broth and fluffy dumplings make this old-fashioned chicken and dumplings pure comfort food.

3   split, bone-in, skin-on chicken breasts
    (about 2½ pounds)
Kosher salt and freshly ground black pepper
1   tablespoon olive oil
1   small yellow onion, peeled and quartered
¾   cup thinly sliced celery (about 3 ribs)
¾   cup carrots cut on the bias about ¼-inch
    thick
6   cups chicken stock

1   cup all-purpose flour
2   teaspoons baking powder
½   teaspoon salt
¼   teaspoon black pepper
¼   cup plus 1 teaspoon milk
1   large egg
½   teaspoon dried thyme
½   teaspoon finely sliced fresh chives
3   tablespoons heavy cream

▶ Rinse the chicken and pat dry with paper towels. Generously season the chicken with salt and pepper. In a large stockpot or Dutch oven over medium-high heat, warm the oil until a few droplets of water sizzle when carefully sprinkled in the pot. Cook the chicken, turning occasionally, until nicely browned on all sides, about 6 minutes. Transfer the chicken to a plate and reserve.

▶ Drain all but about 1 tablespoon of fat from the pot. Add the onion, celery, and carrots. Cook, stirring often, until soft, about 5 minutes. Add the stock and, over high heat, bring the sauce to a boil. Season with salt and pepper to taste. Return the chicken to the pot. Reduce the heat to medium-low, cover, and simmer until the chicken is tender and cooked through, about 45 minutes. Reduce the heat to low. Using a slotted spoon, transfer the cooked chicken and vegetables to a large mixing bowl. Discard the onion. Once the chicken is cool enough to handle, remove and discard the bones and the skin. Shred the chicken meat into 2-inch pieces.

▶ To make the dumplings, combine the flour, baking powder, ½ teaspoon of salt, and ¼ teaspoon of pepper in a medium mixing bowl. In a small bowl whisk together the milk, egg, thyme, and chives. Using a fork, stir the egg mixture into the flour until just moistened. Gather the dough into a ball and, on a floured work surface, knead the dough once or twice until soft. Using your hand, flatten the dough into a rectangle about ½-inch thick, and cut it into 12 equal pieces.

▶ Over high heat, bring the broth back to a simmer. Reduce the heat to medium-high. Whisk in the heavy cream. Drop the dumplings into the simmering mixture and simmer until the dumplings are puffed and cooked through, about 10 minutes. Return the chicken and vegetables to the pot. Cook until the chicken is warm, about 2 minutes. Serve immediately.

Serves 6.

Back-to-the-Basics: I add a little heavy cream to the broth at the end to give it an extra creamy richness. You can omit the heavy cream if you prefer.

 Cooking Tip: To cut "on the bias" means to cut on a diagonal angle (roughly about 45 degrees). It gives a more elegant presentation than slicing straight across.

Chicken Cordon Bleu

The words cordon bleu *conjure up images of fancy cooking schools and haughty French chefs. But in reality, this cheesy, stuffed chicken dish is a cinch to make at home.*

2 tablespoons olive oil, plus extra to grease the pan
1 cup Italian-style bread crumbs
4 boneless, skinless chicken breasts (about 1½ pounds)

Kosher salt and freshly ground black pepper
8 thin slices Swiss cheese
4 thin slices baked ham

▶ Preheat the oven to 350 degrees. Lightly grease the bottom of a baking dish with olive oil. Place the bread crumbs in a shallow bowl and set aside.

▶ Rinse the chicken and pat dry with paper towels. Place the chicken in between two pieces of wax paper or plastic wrap and, using a meat mallet or rolling pin, pound to ¼-inch thickness. Generously season both sides of the chicken breasts with salt and pepper. On each breast, layer 2 slices of cheese and 1 slice of ham.

Tightly roll up each breast and secure with a toothpick. Drizzle the breasts lightly with olive oil and roll them in the bread crumbs to lightly, but evenly, coat. Place the chicken, seam side down, into the prepared baking dish and transfer to the oven. Bake until browned and cooked through, about 30 minutes. To serve, remove the toothpicks and slice crosswise. Serve hot.

Serves 4.

Cooking Tip: This is the basic cooking technique for stuffing a chicken breast. Experiment with some of your favorite ingredients. For an Italian twist, I like to substitute prosciutto, spinach, and mozzarella.

Do Ahead: The chicken can be prepped the night before, tightly wrapped in plastic wrap, and refrigerated.

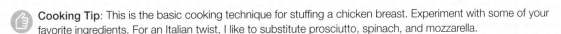

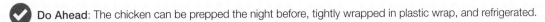

Freezes Well: This dish also freezes well uncooked. Wrap each breast tightly in plastic wrap and then in a layer of foil before freezing. Thaw before baking.

Chicken Enchiladas with Salsa Verde

Salsa verde is a tangy green salsa made from tomatillos instead of tomatoes. It is possible to make your own, but it's more convenient, and equally tasty, to use the jarred variety.

3   cups shredded cooked chicken
1   cup sour cream
2   jars (16-ounce) salsa verde, divided
Kosher salt and freshly ground black pepper

12 small (4-inch) corn tortillas
2   cups shredded Monterey Jack cheese, divided

▶ Preheat the oven to 350 degrees.

▶ Place the cooked chicken in a medium mixing bowl. Add the sour cream and 1 cup of the salsa verde and toss to evenly coat. Season with salt and pepper to taste. Set aside.

▶ Evenly spread 1 cup of the remaining salsa verde over the bottom of a 9- x 13-inch baking dish. Warm the corn tortillas according to the package directions. In the center of each tortilla, place about 2 generous spoonfuls of the chicken mixture, sprinkle with a generous pinch of the cheese, and roll the tortilla to enclose the filling. Place the enchilada seam side down in the pan. Repeat with the remaining tortillas. Pour the remaining salsa verde over the top of the enchiladas and sprinkle with the remaining cheese. Bake, uncovered, until the cheese is melted and bubbly on top, about 30 minutes. Serve hot.

Serves 6.

 Cooking Tip: In order to make the tortillas pliable enough to roll, you need to warm them. Warm corn tortillas on an ungreased skillet over medium-high heat for 10 seconds on each side or by wrapping up 4 to 6 tortillas between two damp paper towels and microwaving for 30 seconds.

Chicken Parmesan

This dish is a favorite at my house. For the adults, I serve it as I describe below. But for the kids, I sometimes cut the chicken into strips and then serve the tomato sauce as a dipping sauce.

1/3 cup all-purpose flour	2 tablespoons olive oil
Kosher salt and freshly ground black pepper	2 cups Basic Tomato Sauce (see page 230 for the recipe)
1 large egg, lightly beaten	1 cup shredded mozzarella cheese
3/4 cup Italian-style bread crumbs	
3/4 cup grated Parmesan cheese	
4 boneless, skinless chicken breasts (about 1 1/2 pounds)	

▸ Preheat the oven to 395 degrees.

▸ Place the flour in a shallow bowl and generously season with salt and pepper. Place the beaten egg in another shallow bowl. Combine the bread crumbs and the Parmesan cheese in a third shallow bowl.

▸ Rinse the chicken and pat dry with paper towels. Place the chicken in between two pieces of wax paper or plastic wrap and, using a meat mallet or rolling pin, pound to 1/4-inch thickness. Generously season both sides of the chicken breasts with salt and pepper. Lightly dredge both sides of the chicken in the seasoned flour, shaking off the excess. Next dip the chicken in the egg wash to coat completely, letting the excess drip off. Then dredge the chicken through the Parmesan bread crumbs, evenly coating on both sides.

▸ In a large ovenproof skillet over medium-high heat, warm the oil until a few droplets of water sizzle when carefully sprinkled in the skillet. Place the chicken in the skillet and cook until golden on both sides, about 3 minutes per side. Transfer to the oven and bake until cooked through, about 10 to 12 minutes.

▸ Remove from the oven and spoon the tomato sauce over the chicken breasts. Sprinkle with the mozzarella cheese and return to the oven until the cheese is just melted, about 2 minutes. Serve immediately.

Serves 4.

 Cooking Tip: Use a nonstick skillet so you do not lose any of the golden crust.

 Time-Saving Tip: You can substitute store-bought marinara tomato sauce for the homemade version.

Chicken Pot Pie

Nothing says comfort food like chicken pot pie. Chicken and vegetables in a rich and creamy sauce topped off with a flaky crust makes for a satisfying one-dish meal.

3 split, bone-in, skin-on chicken breasts (about 2 1/2 pounds)
2 tablespoons olive oil
Kosher salt and freshly ground black pepper
3 cups water
1 cup peeled and finely sliced carrots (about 4 carrots)
1 cup peeled and diced white potatoes (about 1 large potato)
1/2 cup finely diced yellow onion (1 small onion)

1 cup fresh or frozen peas
4 tablespoons unsalted butter
4 tablespoons all-purpose flour, plus extra for rolling out the dough
2 cups chicken stock
1 cup heavy cream
1 teaspoon poultry seasoning
2 unbaked pie crusts (9-inch), homemade or store-bought
1 large egg, lightly beaten

▶ Preheat the oven to 375 degrees.

▶ Rinse the chicken and pat dry with paper towels. Rub the chicken with the olive oil and generously season with salt and pepper. Place on a baking sheet and roast until cooked through, about 35 to 40 minutes. Set aside until cool enough to handle, then remove and discard the bones and the skin. Cut the chicken meat into large dice. (You should have about 3 to 4 cups of chicken.)

▶ While the chicken is roasting, in a medium saucepan over high heat, bring the water to a boil. Add the carrots, potato, onion, and peas, and cook until crisp-tender, about 8 minutes. Drain well and set aside.

▶ Raise the oven temperature to 395 degrees.

▶ In another large pot, melt the butter over medium-low heat. Add the 4 tablespoons flour and whisk until the mixture is golden brown, about 4 to 5 minutes. Whisk in the chicken stock and cream. Add the poultry seasoning and season with salt and pepper to taste. Cook, stirring often, until thickened, about 5 minutes. Add the chicken, carrots, potato, onion, and peas. Stir to combine. Adjust the seasonings as necessary.

▶ Pour the filling into a 9- x 13-inch baking dish. On a lightly floured surface, place the two pie crusts on top of each other. Roll the dough until it is big enough to cover the baking dish. Place the pie crust over the top. Flute the edges, if desired, and cut slits in the top for steam to escape. Brush the crust with the beaten egg. In case of overflow, place the baking dish on a rimmed baking sheet. Bake until golden brown, about 35 to 45 minutes.

Serves 8.

Cooking Tips: Sometimes I top the filling with biscuits rather than with pie crust. For a shortcut, you can use canned biscuits, but I prefer homemade. Just add the biscuits 15 minutes into the cooking time to prevent burning.

Poultry seasoning is an aromatic blend of herbs. If you don't have this seasoning in your pantry, you can make your own by grinding together 1 tablespoon each of dried rosemary, dried sage, dried thyme, and dried marjoram in a spice grinder or mini food processor. Or you can simply season your pot pie filling with a pinch of each.

 Time-Saving Tip: Short on time? Pick up a rotisserie chicken at your local grocery store for this recipe.

 Do Ahead: Pot pies can be made a day in advance. If doing so, either top with the pie crust just before baking or make sure the pie filling is completely cooled before topping with the uncooked pie crust. It also freezes well unbaked either with or without the pie crust.

 Variation: Peas, carrots, and potatoes are the most common pot pie vegetables, but feel free to substitute your favorites. Green beans, parsnips, and sweet potatoes are all delicious additions to a pot pie.

 Freezes Well.

See picture on page 22.

Creamy Garlic Chicken

Mellowed by the slow cooking, the garlic in this dish produces a delectable sauce that will turn everyone at your table into a garlic lover.

4	split, bone-in, skin-on chicken breasts (about 3 pounds)		2	tablespoons cognac
	Kosher salt and freshly ground black pepper		1	cup dry white wine
1	tablespoon unsalted butter		1	tablespoon fresh thyme leaves
2	tablespoons olive oil		2	tablespoons all-purpose flour
2	heads of garlic, separated into cloves and peeled (about 20 cloves)		2	tablespoons heavy cream

▶ Rinse the chicken and pat dry with paper towels. Generously season with salt and pepper. In a large stockpot or Dutch oven over medium-high heat, warm the oil and butter until a few droplets of water sizzle when carefully sprinkled in the pot. Cook the chicken, turning occasionally, until nicely browned on all sides, about 6 minutes. Transfer the chicken to a plate and reserve.

▶ Drain all but about 1 tablespoon of fat from the pot. Add the garlic and cook, stirring occasionally, until lightly browned and fragrant, about 4 minutes. Add the cognac, white wine, and thyme. Over high heat, bring the mixture to a boil. Return the chicken to the pot. Reduce the heat to medium-low, cover, and simmer until the chicken is cooked through, about 30 minutes.

▶ Using tongs or a slotted spoon, transfer the chicken to a plate and cover with foil to keep warm. Whisk the flour into the sauce. Over medium-high heat, bring the sauce back to a boil. Whisk in the heavy cream and cook until the sauce slightly thickens, about 3 minutes. Season with salt and pepper to taste.

▶ To serve, pour the sauce over the chicken and serve hot.

Serves 4.

 Cooking Tip: Looking for a quick and easy way to peel garlic? Drop the separated but unpeeled garlic into a pot of boiling water. Cook for a minute and then drain. The skins will pop right off with no effort at all.

Potato Chip Chicken Tenders

Old-fashioned fried chicken is good, but I think my version raises the bar.

1/2   cup all-purpose flour
Kosher salt and freshly ground black pepper
2   large eggs, lightly beaten
1   bag (11-ounce) potato chips, crushed

4   boneless, skinless chicken breasts
(about 1 1/2 pounds)
Vegetable oil, for frying

▶ Preheat the oven to 350 degrees. Line a baking sheet with parchment paper.

▶ Place the flour in a shallow bowl and season generously with salt and pepper. Place the beaten eggs in another shallow bowl. Leave the crushed potato chips in the bag. (This way you don't dirty another dish!)

▶ Rinse the chicken and pat dry with paper towels. Slice each chicken breast lengthwise into 4 or 5 strips. Generously season the chicken with salt and pepper. Working in small batches, lightly dredge both sides of the chicken in the seasoned flour, shaking off the excess. Next dip the chicken in the egg wash to coat completely, letting the excess drip off. Then dredge the chicken through the crushed potato chips, evenly coating on all sides. Place the prepared chicken on a baking sheet or cutting board.

▶ In a large stockpot or Dutch oven, pour enough oil so that approximately 1 inch of oil covers the entire surface. Over medium-high heat, warm the oil until a few droplets of water sizzle when carefully sprinkled in the pot. In batches, so as not to overcrowd the pot, cook the chicken until golden brown, about 3 minutes per side. Transfer the chicken to a baking sheet lined with parchment paper. Transfer to the oven and bake until the chicken is cooked through, about 15 to 20 minutes. Serve warm.

Serves 4 to 6.

 Cooking Tip: I like to serve this with my homemade honey mustard sauce. Just whisk together equal amounts prepared yellow mustard, whole-grain Dijon mustard, and mayonnaise. Add honey to taste.

 Freezes Well: The prepared but uncooked chicken tenders freeze well. To prevent sticking, freeze the chicken tenders in a single layer on a baking sheet before placing them in a container or freezer bag. When you are ready to cook the chicken tenders, no need to thaw. You can fry them frozen, about 4 minutes per side.

Roast Chicken with Pan Gravy

There is nothing that makes your kitchen smell as homey as a chicken roasting in the oven. I usually make one each week. We have roast chicken the first night, and then I use the leftover cooked chicken in salads or other dishes throughout the week.

1 roasting chicken (3 to 4 pounds)	4 sprigs fresh thyme
Kosher salt and freshly ground black pepper	3 tablespoons unsalted butter, softened
1 yellow onion, peeled and quartered	1 1/2 cups water
1 lemon, cut in half	

▶ Preheat the oven to 395 degrees.

▶ Remove and discard the giblets and any excess fat from the chicken cavity. Rinse the chicken, inside and out, with cold water and pat dry with paper towels. Generously season the inside cavity with salt and pepper.

▶ Stuff the inside of the chicken with the onion quarters, lemon halves, and fresh thyme. Place the chicken in a roasting pan, tucking the tips of the wings under the bottom to keep them from burning. Bring the legs together, cross them, and tie together with kitchen twine. Evenly spread the butter over the skin of the whole bird. Generously season the skin with salt and pepper.

▶ Bake, basting the chicken with the pan juices every 20 minutes, until the skin is golden brown and the juices run clear, about 1 1/2 to 2 hours. (Another trick to knowing if your bird is done is if the leg is loose in the socket when twisted.)

▶ Transfer the chicken to a serving platter or a cutting board with a well. Cover loosely with foil and let the chicken rest for 10 minutes before slicing.

▶ Pour the pan drippings from the roasting pan and discard. Add the water to the roasting pan. Over high heat, bring the water to a boil and stir with a wooden spoon to scrape the browned bits on the bottom. Reduce the heat to medium and simmer until the sauce is reduced in volume by half, about 5 minutes. Season the sauce with salt and pepper to taste. Strain the gravy.

▶ Carve the chicken and serve with the gravy on the side.

Serves 4 to 6.

 Cooking Tip: When roasting chickens, the basic rule of thumb for cooking time is 25 minutes per pound. To be sure the chicken is thoroughly cooked, insert a meat thermometer into the breast. The chicken is cooked when the breast is at least 175 degrees.

Turkey Burgers

The key to a juicy turkey burger is adding ingredients such as cheese and mustard that impart plenty of flavor, as well as much-needed moisture.

¼	cup panko bread crumbs
1	tablespoon milk
1	pound ground turkey (7 percent fat)
½	cup grated sharp white cheddar cheese
¼	cup thinly sliced scallions (about 2 scallions)

3	tablespoons Dijon mustard
	Kosher salt and freshly ground black pepper
2	tablespoons olive oil
4	hamburger buns, split

▸ Preheat the oven to 395 degrees.

▸ In a large mixing bowl combine the bread crumbs and milk until all the milk has been absorbed. Add the ground turkey, cheddar cheese, scallions, and Dijon mustard. Season with salt and pepper to taste. Gently mix together, by hand or with a fork, until well combined. Divide and shape the mixture into 4 patties.

▸ In a large ovenproof skillet over medium-high heat, warm the oil until a few droplets of water sizzle when carefully sprinkled in the skillet. Cook the turkey burgers until well-browned on both sides, about 3 minutes per side. Transfer the skillet to the oven and cook until the turkey burgers are cooked through and no longer pink in the middle, about 8 to 10 minutes.

▸ To serve, toast the buns. Place each burger inside a bun, and garnish as desired. Serve immediately.

Serves 4.

 Cooking Tip: Since turkey is so lean, be sure to use ground turkey that is at least 7 percent fat. Using anything leaner will result in dry burgers.

 Do Ahead: Burgers can be formed, tightly wrapped, and refrigerated for up to 24 hours in advance.

 Freezes Well: Freeze uncooked patties on a baking sheet, then wrap the frozen burgers individually in plastic wrap before placing in a resealable freezer bag. Freezing the burgers separately allows you to defrost as few or as many as you need.

MEAT

Opposite page: Italian Meatloaf (page 66)

Apricot Pork Tenderloin

This is a great last-minute dinner. The pork tenderloin cooks quickly, and the apricot preserves add just the perfect touch of sweetness.

1 pork tenderloin (about 1 1/4 pounds), trimmed
Kosher salt and freshly ground black pepper
2 tablespoons olive oil

1 cup apricot preserves, divided
1 1/2 cups water
1/2 teaspoon dried thyme

▶ Preheat the oven to 395 degrees.

▶ Rinse the pork tenderloin and pat it dry with paper towels. Generously season with salt and pepper. In a large cast-iron or ovenproof skillet over medium-high heat, warm the oil until a few droplets of water sizzle when carefully sprinkled in the skillet. Sear the tenderloin until well-browned on all four sides, about 3 minutes per side. Brush 3/4 cup of apricot preserves over the top and place the pan in the oven to finish cooking the tenderloin, about 15 to 20 minutes. Transfer the tenderloin to a cutting board with a well. Cover loosely with foil and let the pork rest about 5 minutes.

▶ Pour the pan drippings out of the pan and discard. Add the water to the pan. Over high heat, bring the water to a boil. Stir with a wooden spoon to scrape the browned bits off the bottom of the pan. Reduce the heat to medium and simmer until the sauce is reduced by half, about 5 minutes. Stir in the remaining 1/4 cup apricot preserves and thyme. Season with salt and pepper to taste. Simmer just until the apricot preserves have melted into the sauce, about 2 minutes.

▶ Thinly slice the tenderloin and serve with the sauce spooned over the top.

Serves 4.

 Cooking Tip: If you are unsure if the pork (or any other meat) is fully cooked, use a meat thermometer. Pork is safe to eat when it is cooked to an internal temperature of 155 to 160 degrees.

 Back-to-the-Basics: Leave off the apricot preserves for a simple yet tasty tenderloin.

Beef Tostadas

A tostada is basically an open-face crunchy taco. This recipe is one of my husband's favorite things to make. His special trick is to spread a thicker layer of the refried beans around the edges, almost like creating a well, to keep the other toppings from falling off.

1	tablespoon vegetable oil, plus extra for frying the tortillas
1	pound ground beef
1/4	cup finely diced yellow onions (1 small onion)
	Kosher salt and freshly ground black pepper
1	can (15-ounce) refried beans
8	small (4-inch) corn tortillas

1/2	cup sour cream
1	bag (8-ounce) shredded iceberg lettuce
1	cup salsa
1	cup shredded cheddar or Monterey Jack cheese
	Sliced pickled jalapeños (optional)

▶ In a large skillet over medium-high heat, warm the oil until a few droplets of water sizzle when carefully sprinkled in the skillet. Add the ground beef and onion and cook, stirring with a wooden spoon to break up the beef, until the meat is browned and cooked through, about 5 minutes. Season with salt and pepper to taste. Cover to keep warm.

▶ In a small saucepan, warm the refried beans over medium-low heat. Season to taste with salt and pepper. Cover to keep warm.

▶ In a large stockpot, pour enough oil so that you have a 1/4-inch layer of oil. Warm the oil on medium-high heat until a few droplets of water sizzle when carefully sprinkled in the pot or a thermometer reads 375 degrees. One at a time, fry the tortillas until crisp and golden brown on both sides, about 30 seconds to 1 minute per side. Use metal tongs to lift the tortilla out of the pan, draining the excess oil as you do so. Transfer the tortillas to a paper towel-lined plate to drain.

▶ To serve, spread 2 or 3 tablespoons of refried beans evenly over each tortilla, followed by 1 tablespoon of sour cream. Add the ground beef. Garnish with salsa, cheese, and a small handful of lettuce. Top with jalapeños if desired. Serve immediately.

Serves 4.

 Cooking Tip: If the oil is not hot enough, the tortillas will not get crispy. For best results when frying, the oil should be heated to 375 degrees. If you do not have a thermometer, you can also tell if the oil is hot enough if bubbles form around the tortilla when you first add it to the hot oil.

 Variation: Chicken can easily be substituted for the ground beef. For a vegetarian version, omit the meat and add grilled veggies or sliced avocado.

Boeuf Bourguignon

If you've seen the movie Julie & Julia, *you know that Julia Child's rendition of this classic French dish is what got her first book deal. This version is from the kitchen of another talented chef, my sister Susan.*

4 pounds boneless beef chuck roast, trimmed and cut into 2-inch cubes
Kosher salt and freshly ground black pepper
2 tablespoons olive oil
5 slices bacon, cut into 1/2-inch pieces
1 cup finely diced yellow onion (1 large onion)
1 1/2 cups thinly sliced carrots (about 5 small carrots)
6 sprigs fresh thyme
3 bay leaves

3 cloves garlic, minced
1 can (14.5-ounce) whole tomatoes with juice
1 bottle (750 ml) good red wine (preferably Pinot Noir or Burgundy)
2 cups chicken stock
2 tablespoons unsalted butter
2 cups button mushrooms, trimmed and quartered
1 1/2 cups frozen small whole white pearl onions

▶ Preheat the oven to 250 degrees.

▶ Pat the beef dry with paper towels and generously season with salt and pepper. In a large Dutch oven or stockpot over medium-high heat, warm the oil until a few droplets of water sizzle when carefully sprinkled in the pot. In two batches, so as to not overcrowd the pot, cook the meat until nicely browned on all sides, about 8 minutes per batch. Transfer the meat to a plate.

▶ Drain all but 1 tablespoon of fat from the pot. Add the bacon and cook over medium heat until crispy, about 3 to 4 minutes. Add the onion, carrots, thyme, bay leaves, and garlic. Cook, stirring, until the onions are soft, about 5 minutes.

▶ Add the tomatoes, red wine, and chicken stock and stir to combine. Return the beef to the pot. Season with salt and pepper to taste. Bring the mixture to a boil, cover, and place in the oven. Cook until the beef is fork tender, about 2 hours. Remove from the oven and place on the stove over low heat to keep warm. Discard the bay leaves and cover.

▶ In a medium skillet over medium-high heat, melt the butter. Add the mushrooms and sauté until softened and golden, about 4 minutes. Add the cooked mushrooms and frozen onions to the stew. Over medium-high heat, bring the stew back to a boil and adjust the seasonings as needed. Serve hot.

Serves 6.

Time-Saving Tip: You can use fresh pearl onions in this recipe, but they need to be peeled and cooked first. Frozen onions are equally delicious and save you 15 to 20 minutes of preparation time.

Do Ahead: This stew can be made a day or two in advance. In fact, I think it may be even better the second day. Just reheat the stew on your stovetop over medium-low heat.

Freezes Well.

Braised Short Ribs

I love this dish! Not only are the tender short ribs satisfyingly delicious, but I can do the prep work and stick the short ribs in the oven hours before my guests arrive.

6   bone-in, individually cut beef short ribs
    (about 4 to 6 pounds)
Kosher salt and freshly ground black pepper
3   tablespoons olive oil
1   cup diced carrots (about 3 carrots)
1   cup diced yellow onion (about 1 large onion)
1/2 cup thinly sliced celery (about 2 ribs)
4   cloves garlic, minced

2   cups full-bodied red wine (such as a Syrah
    or Merlot)
1   can (14.5-ounce) whole tomatoes with juice
1   cup chicken stock
3   sprigs fresh thyme
3   sprigs fresh rosemary
6 to 8 cups cooked stone-ground grits (see page
    229 for the recipe) or polenta, warm

▶ Preheat the oven to 375 degrees.

▶ Pat the beef dry with paper towels and generously season with salt and pepper. In a large Dutch oven or stockpot over medium-high heat, warm the oil until a few droplets of water sizzle when carefully sprinkled in the pot. In two batches so as not to overcrowd the pot, cook the meat until nicely browned on all sides, about 8 minutes per batch. Transfer the meat to a plate.

▶ Drain all but 1 tablespoon of fat from the pot. Add the carrots, onion, celery, and garlic. Cook until soft,

about 5 minutes. Stir in the red wine, tomatoes, chicken stock, thyme, and rosemary.

▶ Over high heat, bring the sauce to a boil and return the meat to the pan. Season with salt and pepper to taste. Cover and place in the oven. Cook until the beef is fork tender, about 2 hours. Remove from the oven.

▶ To serve, place the short ribs over warm stone-ground grits or polenta. Spoon the sauce over the top. Serve warm.

Serves 6.

 Do Ahead: Short ribs can be made the day before. To reheat, just warm the short ribs in the sauce on the stove-top or in the oven.

 Freezes Well.

Carnitas Pork Tacos

In Mexican cuisine, carnitas is a deliciously tender braised pork dish. Some recipes call for simmering the meat for hours on the stovetop, but I just throw all the ingredients in a slow cooker in the morning, and come dinnertime, it's ready to go.

5 pounds pork butt, trimmed
Kosher salt and freshly ground black pepper
3 tablespoons ground cumin
2 cans (10-ounce) diced tomatoes with green chiles (or 2$^1/_2$ cups jarred tomato salsa)

12 small (4-inch) flour tortillas, warmed per package directions
$^3/_4$ cup sour cream
$^3/_4$ cup tomato salsa
$^1/_4$ cup fresh cilantro leaves

▶ Rinse the pork and pat dry with paper towels. Generously season with salt and pepper and sprinkle with the cumin. Place the pork in a slow cooker and pour the tomatoes over the top. Cover and cook on low until fork tender, about 8 to 10 hours.

▶ Transfer the cooked pork to a cutting board with a well. Remove and discard the fatty portions and any bones. Pull the pork apart and return it to the cooking liquid in the slow cooker to keep it warm and juicy.

▶ To serve, assemble the tacos by placing the pulled pork in the center of the warmed tortillas. Garnish with the sour cream, salsa, and cilantro. Serve warm.

Serves 6 to 8.

 Cooking Tips: Slow cookers cook best when the lid remains tightly in place. Opening the lid often will require additional cooking time. Please refer to your machine's instructions.

You need at least a 3$^1/_2$ quart slow cooker for this recipe.

 Variation: This tender pulled pork would also be delicious tossed with your favorite barbecue sauce. Strain off the cooking liquid before tossing the pork with the barbecue sauce.

 Freezes Well.

Cheeseburger Pie

I had to laugh when my good friend Gay Landaiche gave me this recipe. Cheeseburger Pie?! Whoever heard of such a thing? But Gay is a great cook, so I gave it a try. And just as she said it would be, this dish was a big hit for my whole family!

1	unbaked pie crust (9-inch), homemade or store-bought
1	tablespoon vegetable oil
1	pound ground beef
1/2	cup finely diced yellow onion (1 small onion)
2	tablespoons all-purpose flour

1	tablespoon Worcestershire sauce
	Kosher salt and freshly ground black pepper
2	large eggs
1	cup small-curd cottage cheese
2	medium tomatoes, thinly sliced
1	cup shredded sharp cheddar cheese

▶ Preheat the oven to 395 degrees.

▶ Place the pie crust in a deep-dish pie pan. Flute the edges, if desired. Place the prepared pie crust in the refrigerator until ready to fill.

▶ In a large skillet over medium-high heat, warm the oil until a few droplets of water sizzle when carefully sprinkled in the skillet. Add the ground beef and onion. Cook, breaking up the beef with a wooden spoon, until the meat is browned and cooked through, about 5 minutes. Transfer the meat and onions to a colander and drain off the excess fat. In a large bowl, stir the meat and onions with the flour and Worcestershire sauce. Season with salt and pepper to taste. Spoon the mixture into the prepared pie crust.

▶ In a small bowl stir together the eggs and cottage cheese. Spoon the cottage cheese mixture evenly over the beef. Arrange tomato slices on top of the cottage cheese and sprinkle the cheddar cheese evenly over the top.

▶ Bake until set and the cheese has melted, about 30 minutes.

Serves 6.

 Cooking Tip: Feel free to serve with your favorite burger condiments: ketchup, mustard, mayonnaise, even pickles!

Slow Cooker Beef Stew

This is one of my favorite workday dishes. I place everything in the slow cooker before I head off to work, and when I come home, I have a delicious home-cooked meal waiting to be served.

4   pounds beef chuck roast, trimmed and cut into 2-inch cubes
Kosher salt and freshly ground black pepper
2   tablespoons olive oil
1/2   cup good red wine (such as a Merlot or Syrah)

1   can (28-ounce) whole tomatoes with juice
4   cloves garlic, minced
1 1/2   cups baby carrots
2   bay leaves

▸ Pat the meat dry with a paper towel and generously season with salt and pepper.

▸ In a large cast-iron skillet over medium-high heat, warm the oil until a few droplets of water sizzle when carefully sprinkled in the skillet. In two batches so as not to over-crowd the skillet, cook the meat until nicely browned on all sides, about 8 minutes per batch. Transfer the meat to the slow cooker.

▸ Pour the red wine into the skillet, stirring with a wooden spoon to scrape the brown bits off the bottom, to deglaze the pan. Pour the wine mixture into the slow cooker.

▸ Add the tomatoes to the slow cooker, breaking them up with a spoon or fork. Add the garlic, carrots, and bay leaves. Cover and cook until fork tender, on high for about 5 to 6 hours or on low for about 7 to 8 hours. Adjust seasonings as needed. Discard the bay leaves. Serve warm.

Serves 6 to 8.

Cooking Tips: If you do not have a slow cooker, you can still make this dish. Follow all the directions above, and place the ingredients in a Dutch oven or heavy stock pot with a lid and bake in a 250-degree oven for 3 hours.

You need at least a 3 1/2 quart slow cooker for this recipe.

Back-to-the-Basics: I like the flavor that the wine imparts to this dish. But if you don't have a bottle on hand, just deglaze the skillet with 1/2 cup of water instead.

Freezes Well.

Garlic and Rosemary Lamb Chops

I learned how to make this dish when I lived in France. I consider it my "French comfort food" since it brings back memories of delicious meals in Parisian bistros. I serve it with potatoes au gratin and haricots verts.

1/2	cup good red wine (preferably Pinot Noir or Burgundy)
4	cloves garlic, minced
2	tablespoons chopped fresh rosemary leaves

8	lamb loin chops (4 ounces each)
	Kosher salt and freshly ground black pepper
2	tablespoons olive oil

▸ In a small bowl whisk together the red wine, garlic, and rosemary. Place the lamb chops in a resealable plastic bag and pour the marinade over them. Move the chops around in the bag to coat them well. Place in the refrigerator and marinate for 1 hour.

▸ Preheat the oven to 395 degrees.

▸ Remove the lamb chops from the marinade, drain off any excess, and discard the marinade. Let the lamb chops come to room temperature before cooking, about 20 minutes. Generously season the lamb chops with salt and pepper on both sides.

▸ In a large cast-iron skillet over medium-high heat, warm the oil until a few droplets of water sizzle when carefully sprinkled in the skillet. Sear the lamb chops until well-browned on both sides, about 3 minutes per side. Place the chops in the oven until medium-rare, about 8 minutes, or until desired doneness. Serve immediately.

Serves 4.

 Cooking Tip: Balsamic vinegar or red wine vinegar can be substituted for the red wine.

 Do Ahead: Want to get dinner started before heading off to work? You can marinate the lamb chops up to 10 hours in advance.

Italian Meatloaf

I was never a huge fan of meatloaf until I tasted this version from Emily Nokes Martin, a talented personal chef in my hometown of Memphis, Tennessee. No more bland and dry meatloaf for me. What sets this recipe apart is the use of both ground beef and ground pork, as well as the flavorful seasonings.

2	ounces pancetta (or bacon), thinly sliced and cut into 1/4-inch strips
1	tablespoon olive oil
1/2	cup finely diced yellow onion (1 small onion)
1/2	cup finely diced red bell pepper (1 small pepper)
1	clove garlic, minced
1/4	cup shredded carrots (1 carrot)
1	large egg
3	tablespoons milk
1	cup Italian-style bread crumbs

1	tablespoon herbs de Provence
1	tablespoon dried basil leaves
1	tablespoon Worcestershire sauce
1	tablespoon Dijon mustard
2	tablespoons tomato paste
1	pound ground beef
1/2	pound ground pork
1/4	cup finely diced roasted red bell peppers, jarred or homemade (see page 233)
1/2	cup shredded mozzarella cheese
Kosher salt and freshly ground black pepper	

▶ Preheat the oven to 350 degrees.

▶ In a large skillet over medium heat, cook the pancetta until evenly browned and crispy. Remove with a slotted spoon and transfer to a paper towel–lined plate. Reserve.

▶ Drain all but 1 tablespoon of fat from the skillet. Add the oil and warm over medium-high heat until a few droplets of water sizzle when carefully sprinkled in the skillet. Add the onion, red bell pepper, garlic, and carrots. Cook, stirring frequently, until the vegetables are soft, about 5 minutes. Set aside to cool.

▶ In a large mixing bowl combine the egg, milk, bread crumbs, herbs de Provence, dried basil, Worcestershire, mustard, and tomato paste. Stir until well combined. Add the beef, pork, cooled vegetable mixture, roasted red bell peppers, and cheese. Season with salt and pepper to taste. Gently mix together by hand.

▶ Lightly spray a baking sheet with cooking spray. Form the meatloaf mixture into a log, about 6 inches long and 4 inches wide. Bake until the meatloaf is firm, about 1 to 1 1/2 hours. Remove from the oven and let stand for 5 minutes before slicing. Serve warm.

Serves 6.

 Cooking Tips: The secret to a moist, tender meatloaf is to use a light touch when combining the ingredients. Overmixing compacts the meat, leading to dry, tough results.

If you want to make sure that the meatloaf is seasoned to your liking, cook a tablespoon size patty in a skillet until cooked through. Taste and adjust seasonings as desired.

Save cleaning time by lining the baking sheet with parchment paper before cooking.

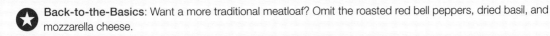 **Back-to-the-Basics**: Want a more traditional meatloaf? Omit the roasted red bell peppers, dried basil, and mozzarella cheese.

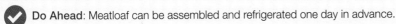 **Do Ahead**: Meatloaf can be assembled and refrigerated one day in advance.

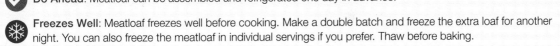 **Freezes Well**: Meatloaf freezes well before cooking. Make a double batch and freeze the extra loaf for another night. You can also freeze the meatloaf in individual servings if you prefer. Thaw before baking.

See picture on page 48.

Peppered Filets with a Grainy Mustard Cream Sauce

I think the best way to prepare a filet is with a cast-iron skillet and an oven. First I sear the meat on the stovetop to give it a nice crust, and then I finish the steak in the oven. The results are a more tender and juicy steak than any I have had off of a grill.

4	filet mignons, cut 1¹/₄-inches thick each
	Kosher salt
2	tablespoons coarsely ground black pepper
1	tablespoon olive oil
1	shallot, peeled and finely minced

¹/₄	cup brandy
1	tablespoon whole-grain Dijon mustard
¹/₂	cup heavy cream
	Freshly ground pepper

▶ Preheat the oven to 395 degrees.

▶ Pat the beef dry with paper towels. Generously season the beef with salt. Evenly press the coarse pepper on both flat sides of the filets. In a large cast-iron skillet over medium-high heat, warm the oil until a few droplets of water sizzle when carefully sprinkled in the skillet. Sear the steaks until well browned on both sides, about 3 minutes per side. Place the steaks in the oven to finish cooking, about 8 minutes for medium-rare. (For medium, cook the steak an additional 2 to 3 minutes.) Transfer the steaks to a plate and cover with foil to keep warm.

▶ Pour all but 1 tablespoon of fat from the skillet. Add the shallots and sauté over medium heat until soft, about 3 minutes. Add the brandy and simmer, uncovered until the liquor has almost evaporated, about 3 minutes. Whisk in the mustard and heavy cream. Bring the sauce to a simmer and season with salt and pepper to taste. Serve the steaks hot with the sauce.

Serves 4.

 Cooking Tips: For a milder sauce, you can substitute traditional Dijon mustard for the whole-grain variety.

 Back-to-the-Basics: I like the flavor that the brandy imparts to this sauce. You can substitute bourbon or cognac if you prefer. Or just omit the alcohol completely.

Smothered Pork Chops

This delicious, old-fashioned recipe is from my dear mom. Slow cooking turns tough pork chops into a fork-tender treat.

4	thinly sliced center-cut pork chops (about 1 1/4 pounds)	1	cup thinly sliced yellow onion (1 large onion)
	Kosher salt and freshly ground black pepper	1	can (10 3/4-ounce) cream of celery soup
1	tablespoon olive oil	1	cup water

▶ Pat the pork chops dry with a paper towel and generously season with salt and pepper. In a large saucepan over medium-high heat, warm the oil until a few droplets of water sizzle when carefully sprinkled in the pan. Sear the meat until nicely browned on both sides, about 4 minutes per side. Transfer the meat to a plate and reserve.

▶ Drain all but about 1 tablespoon of fat from the pan. Add the onions and sauté until soft, about 5 minutes. Add the soup and water, and stir to combine. Over high heat, bring the mixture to a boil. Reduce the heat to medium-low. Season with salt and pepper to taste. Return the meat to the pan. Cover and simmer until the meat is tender, about 45 minutes. Adjust seasonings as needed. Serve the pork chops hot with the sauce ladled on top.

Serves 4.

 Cooking Tip: You can use either bone-in or boneless pork chops for this recipe.

Veal Piccata

Veal piccata has always been one of my husband's favorite things to order at Italian restaurants. I was pleasantly surprised to learn how easy this dish is to make at home.

8	thinly sliced veal scallops, about 1/4-inch thick
	Kosher salt and freshly ground pepper
1	tablespoon olive oil
1/2	cup chicken stock
1/2	cup dry white wine

2	tablespoons freshly squeezed lemon juice
3	tablespoons unsalted butter, at room temperature
2	tablespoons drained capers
1	lemon, thinly sliced into rounds

▶ Pat the veal dry with paper towels and generously season with salt and pepper.

▶ In a large skillet over medium-high heat, warm the oil until a few droplets of water sizzle when carefully sprinkled in the skillet. In several batches so as to not overcrowd the skillet, cook the meat until nicely browned, about 3 minutes per side. Be careful not to overcook. Transfer the meat to a plate and tent with foil to keep warm. Drain all of the fat from the pan.

▶ For the sauce, add the stock, wine, and lemon juice to the skillet and cook over medium-high heat, stirring with a wooden spoon to scrape up the browned bits from the bottom, until the sauce is reduced by half, about 3 minutes. Whisk in the butter. Stir in the capers and sliced lemons and cook until warmed through, about 1 to 2 minutes. Season with salt and pepper to taste.

▶ To serve, place two veal scallops on each plate and spoon the sauce over the top.

Serves 4.

 Cooking Tip: You can make this recipe with chicken. Substitute 4 skinless, boneless chicken breasts for the veal scallops. Place the chicken breasts between two sheets of wax paper and lightly pound until they are about 1/4-inch thick.

SEAFOOD

Opposite page: Fish Tacos (page 80)

Blackened Catfish

Here in Memphis, Soul Fish Café may be known for its fried catfish, but my favorite item on their menu is the blackened catfish. This is my homemade version, along with the not-so-traditional remoulade they serve on the side to cut the heat.

For the Remoulade Dipping Sauce:

3/4	cup mayonnaise
4	tablespoons ketchup
3	tablespoons freshly squeezed lemon juice
	Kosher salt and freshly ground black pepper
1	tablespoon finely sliced scallions

For the Blackened Catfish:

4	catfish fillets (6 ounces each)
4	tablespoons blackened seasoning
2	tablespoons olive oil

▸ To make the remoulade dipping sauce: In a medium mixing bowl whisk together the mayonnaise, ketchup, and lemon juice. Season with salt and pepper to taste. Stir in the scallions. Cover and refrigerate until ready to serve.

▸ To make the blackened catfish: Season both sides of the fish with the blackened seasoning. In a large skillet over medium-high heat, warm the oil until a few droplets of water sizzle when carefully sprinkled in the skillet. Sear the fish on one side until the meat is well browned and releases easily from the pan, about 4 to 5 minutes. Turn over the fillets and cook to desired doneness, about 5 more minutes. Serve warm with a spoonful of the remoulade dipping sauce.

Serves 4.

 Cooking Tips: If you would like to make your own blackened seasoning, it's really not hard to do. Just whisk together 2 teaspoons paprika and 1/2 teaspoon each of dried thyme, cayenne pepper, granulated sugar, salt, and black pepper. For a little less heat, reduce the amount of cayenne and black pepper. This mixture will store for several weeks, tightly sealed, in your spice cabinet.

This is the basic technique for blackening fish. Feel free to substitute your favorite fish for the catfish. Tilapia, salmon, and swordfish all taste delicious blackened.

 Do-Ahead: The remoulade dipping sauce can be made up to 3 days in advance. Cover and refrigerate until just before serving.

Crawfish Étouffée

Crawfish is probably the one ingredient that most Americans associate with Cajun cooking. The most popular way to eat crawfish is simply boiled, but crawfish étouffée is also a New Orleans favorite. Many versions begin with making a roux, but my grandmother preferred to make this easier recipe.

2	tablespoons unsalted butter
1/4	cup thinly sliced celery (1 rib)
1/2	cup finely diced yellow onion (1 small onion)
1/2	cup finely diced green bell pepper (1 small pepper)
1	clove garlic, minced

1	teaspoon dried thyme
1	pound peeled crawfish tails with fat
3/4	cup water
	Kosher salt and freshly ground black pepper
	Hot sauce (optional)
3	cups cooked white rice, warm

▸ In a large stockpot melt the butter over medium-high heat. Add the celery, onion, bell pepper, and garlic, and sauté until soft, about 5 minutes. Stir in the thyme. Add the crawfish tails and water. Season with salt and pepper to taste. Sauté over medium-low heat until the flavors are melded, about 20 to 25 minutes. Adjust seasonings and add hot sauce, if desired. Serve hot over rice.

Serves 6.

 Cooking Tip: Harvested in the early spring in Southern coastal states, such as Louisiana and Mississippi, crawfish are freshwater crustaceans similar to small lobsters the size of shrimp. Ask your grocer's seafood manager to order them for you, fresh or frozen, in advance. If frozen, thaw overnight in your refrigerator.

Fish Tacos

If you travel to Mexico's Baja region or sunny Southern California, you will find hundreds of restaurants and food stands offering fish tacos. Most often the fish is beer-battered and fried. This version using marinated fish is a lot easier and, in my opinion, even more flavorful.

For the Mango Slaw:

2   cups finely shredded green cabbage
1 1/2 cups finely shredded red cabbage
1   cup diced mango
1/4 cup thinly sliced red onion (about half a small onion)
2   tablespoons seeded and finely diced fresh jalapeños
3   tablespoons freshly squeezed lime juice
2   tablespoons olive oil
Kosher salt and freshly ground black pepper
2   tablespoons coarsely chopped fresh cilantro leaves

For the Avocado Crema:

2   large ripe avocados, peeled, pitted, and coarsely chopped
2   tablespoons freshly squeezed lime juice
1/4 cup sour cream
Kosher salt and freshly ground black pepper

For the Fish Tacos:

1/4 cup plus 1 tablespoon olive oil, divided
2   tablespoons freshly squeezed lime juice
1   clove garlic, minced
1/2 teaspoon chili powder
4   tilapia fillets (6 ounces each)
Kosher salt and freshly ground black pepper
8   small (4-inch) flour tortillas, warmed

▶ To make the mango slaw: In a large mixing bowl combine the green cabbage, red cabbage, mango, red onion, and jalapeño. Add the lime juice and olive oil and toss until well combined. Season to taste with salt and pepper. Fold in the cilantro just before serving.

▶ To make the avocado crema: In a food processor puree the avocado and lime juice until smooth. Blend in the sour cream. Place the crema in a bowl and season with salt and pepper to taste.

▶ To make the fish tacos: In small bowl whisk together 1/4 cup of the olive oil, lime juice, garlic, and chili powder until well blended. Place the tilapia in a shallow dish, and pour the marinade over the fish. Cover and refrigerate for at least 30 minutes or up to 1 hour. Remove the fish from the marinade, drain off any excess, and discard the marinade. Season both sides of the fish with salt and pepper to taste.

▶ In a large skillet over medium-high heat, warm the remaining tablespoon of oil until a few droplets of water sizzle when carefully sprinkled in the skillet. Sear the fish on one side until the meat is well browned and releases easily from the pan, about 4 to 5 minutes. Turn and cook until the fish is cooked through, about 5 minutes more. Transfer the fish to a plate and break into large pieces.

▸ Assemble the tacos by placing the fish (approximately half a fillet per taco) in the center of the tortillas. Garnish with desired amounts of the mango slaw and avocado crema. Serve warm.

Serves 4.

 Time-Saving Tip: Instead of shredding the cabbage for the slaw, pick up a package of shredded angel-hair cole-slaw in your produce department.

 Do Ahead: The slaw can be made up to 2 hours ahead. Store covered in your refrigerator until ready to serve.

 Variation: For a kid friendly version, melt cheddar cheese on a tortilla and top with the seared fish.

See picture on page 74.

Lemon Salmon

If you have ever been nervous about cooking fish, this is the recipe to help you overcome your fear. Baking the salmon in the marinade helps the fish stay tender and moist.

3	tablespoons freshly squeezed lemon juice
3	tablespoons dry white wine
2	tablespoons olive oil
1	shallot, peeled and thinly sliced into rounds
1	lemon, thinly sliced into rounds

4	sprigs fresh thyme
4	boneless salmon fillets (4 to 6 ounces each)
	Kosher salt and freshly ground black pepper

▶ In a shallow, nonreactive baking pan, whisk together the lemon juice, white wine, and oil. Scatter the shallots, lemon slices, and thyme sprigs evenly across the bottom of the pan. Place the salmon filets, flesh side down, into the pan. Cover and refrigerate for at least 30 minutes, but no longer than 1 hour.

▶ Preheat the oven to 385 degrees.

▶ Remove the pan from the refrigerator and let it stand until the fish is room temperature, about 10 minutes on your kitchen counter. Turn the fish over, so the flesh side is up and the skin side is down, and place it back in the marinade. Generously season the fish with salt and pepper. For medium-well salmon, bake the fish in the marinade for 25 to 30 minutes, or bake less until cooked to desired temperature. Serve immediately.

Serves 4.

 Variation: This same lemony marinade is also delicious with other types of light and flaky fish (such as tilapia, orange roughy, and halibut) as well as shellfish (scallops and shrimp). The cooking time may vary slightly depending on thickness.

 Cooking Tip: When marinating anything in an acid, such as lemon juice, wine, or vinegar, be sure to use a nonreactive container. Glass, plastic, ceramic, or stainless steel cookware are all nonreactive and safe to use. (Plastic storage bags are also a great, mess-free option.) Avoid cookware made from aluminum or copper when marinating, because those metals will react with the marinade and give your food a metallic taste.

Pan-Roasted Sea Bass with Chive-Garlic Compound Butter

Pan-roasting is the ideal way to cook fish. Sear the fish until it has a nice golden crust, and then finish cooking it in the oven to keep the fish moist and flaky. I use this same technique with all types of fish.

For the Chive-Garlic Compound Butter:

1 cup unsalted butter (2 sticks), at room temperature
2 tablespoons finely minced fresh chives
1 clove garlic, minced
Pinch of Kosher salt

For the Pan-Roasted Sea Bass:

4 sea bass fillets (4 to 6 ounces each)
Kosher salt and freshly ground black pepper
2 tablespoons olive oil

▶ To make the chive-garlic compound butter: In the bowl of an electric mixer, using the paddle attachment, beat the butter until light and fluffy. Add the chives, garlic, and salt, and mix until thoroughly combined.

▶ Spoon the mixture in the shape of a log onto a piece of parchment paper. Fold the paper over itself. Using your hands, shape the butter into a cylinder about 1¹/₂ inches wide (almost like making a Tootsie Roll™). Once it is shaped, twist the edges to seal it. Place in the freezer to set, about 20 minutes. Refrigerate until ready to serve.

▶ When ready to serve, slice the roll into ¹/₄-inch rounds and remove the parchment. (Only 4 slices of compound butter are needed for this recipe.)

▶ To cook the fish: Preheat the oven to 375 degrees.

▶ Generously season the sea bass with salt and pepper. In a large ovenproof skillet over medium heat, warm the oil until a few water droplets sizzle when carefully sprinkled in the skillet. Sear the sea bass, skin side up, until the meat is well browned and easily releases from pan, about 4 minutes. Flip over and cook until seared, about 1 minute. Transfer the pan to the oven and roast until the fish is medium rare, about 5 minutes, or until desired doneness.

▶ Serve with a slice of compound butter on top.

Serves 4.

 Cooking Tip: Compound butter is simply butter with an added flavor or two mixed in. These butters are a very easy way to look as if you went to a lot of trouble. Compound butter is also delicious with potatoes, corn on the cob, vegetables, and steaks. Experiment with your favorite flavors. Some of my other favorite compound butter combinations are lemon chive, fresh herb, bacon and bleu cheese, and Parmesan and toasted pine nut.

 Do Ahead: The rolled butter can be stored for up to 1 week in the refrigerator and up to 1 month in the freezer.

Shrimp and Grits

This recipe is based on one from Jeff Dunham, the executive chef and owner of The Grove Grill in Memphis. His shrimp and grits are the absolute best. He uses shrimp stock as the base of his sauce, but since I don't usually have that in my kitchen, I use chicken stock.

1   pound large shrimp (16-20 count), peeled and deveined
2   teaspoons Cajun seasoning
2   tablespoons olive oil
2   cloves garlic, minced
1/4   cup finely diced tasso ham
1/4   cup dry white wine
2   tablespoons finely chopped fresh flat-leaf parsley

1/2   cup chicken stock
4   cups Creamy Stone-Ground Grits (see page 229 for the recipe), warm
2   tablespoons unsalted butter
Kosher salt and freshly ground black pepper
2   tablespoons finely sliced scallions (about 1 scallion)

▶ Place the shrimp in a large mixing bowl and toss with the Cajun seasoning.

▶ In a large saucepan over medium-high heat, warm the oil until a few droplets of water sizzle when carefully sprinkled in the pan. Add the shrimp, garlic, and ham, and cook, stirring occasionally, until the shrimp are lightly browned, about 3 to 4 minutes. Add the wine and parsley. Cook until the liquid is reduced in volume by half, about 2 minutes. Add the stock and over high heat, bring the mixture to a boil. Remove from the heat.

▶ Portion the warm grits into the serving bowls and, using tongs, place equal portions of the shrimp over the grits.

▶ Return the sauce to the stovetop and over high heat, bring to a boil. Reduce the heat to medium and cook until reduced in volume by half, about 2 minutes. Remove from the heat and whisk in the butter until melted and well incorporated. Season with salt and pepper to taste. Spoon the sauce over the shrimp and grits, and garnish with the scallions. Serve immediately.

Serves 4.

 Cooking Tip: Tasso ham is a spicy, peppery smoked pork often used in Cajun cooking. If you cannot find it, you can substitute cooked bacon.

Shrimp Scampi

What I like most about this dish is the sauce. Butter and garlic is a marriage made in heaven!

2 pounds large shrimp (16-20 count), peeled and deveined
Kosher salt and freshly ground black pepper
2 tablespoons olive oil
10 tablespoons unsalted butter, divided

4 cloves garlic, minced
1/4 cup dry white wine
1 tablespoon freshly squeezed lemon juice
2 tablespoons finely chopped flat-leaf parsley

▶ Generously season the shrimp with salt and pepper. In a large saucepan over medium-high heat, warm the oil until a few droplets of water sizzle when carefully sprinkled in the pan. Add the shrimp and sauté, turning occasionally, until cooked through, about 4 minutes. Transfer the shrimp to a plate and cover with foil to keep warm.

▶ Reduce the heat to medium-low. Melt 1 tablespoon butter in the same pan that was used for the shrimp. Add the garlic and sauté until it is softened but not browned, about 2 minutes. Add the wine and lemon juice. Raise the heat to high and bring the mixture to a boil. Reduce the heat to medium and simmer until the sauce is reduced by half, about 2 minutes. Reduce the heat to low and whisk in the remaining butter, one tablespoon at a time.

▶ Return the shrimp to the sauce and toss gently to coat. Season with salt and pepper to taste. Garnish with the parsley. Serve hot.

 Cooking Tip: How to peel and devein shrimp 101: Carefully remove the shell from the shrimp. Using a sharp knife, make a shallow incision along the entire length of the back of the shrimp. Remove the intestinal tract with the tip of your knife. Rinse under cold water.

I leave the tails on the shrimp when I peel them to make this dish look as though it came from a restaurant.

 Variation: This basic recipe is also delicious with scallops.

 Time-Saving Tip: Use frozen peeled and deveined shrimp. Defrost by placing them in a bowl in your refrigerator overnight or by running cold water over them in a colander for 10 minutes.

Shrimp, Chicken, and Sausage Jambalaya

"Jambalaya and a crawfish pie and filé gumbo . . . son of a gun, we'll have big fun on the bayou." So goes the refrain of *the famous song by Hank Williams Sr. named after this iconic Louisiana dish. A Creole version of "dirty rice," jambalaya is best enjoyed with a loaf of crusty French bread served on the side.*

3	boneless, skinless chicken breasts (about 1 pound), cut into 1-inch cubes
	Kosher salt and freshly ground black pepper
2	tablespoons olive oil
1	pound smoked Andouille sausage, thinly sliced
1/2	cup finely diced yellow onion (1 small onion)
1/2	cup seeded and finely diced green bell pepper (1 small pepper)
1/4	cup finely diced celery (1 rib)

6	cloves of garlic, minced
1	tablespoon dried oregano
1	tablespoon dried thyme
3	bay leaves
1	can (15-ounce) tomato sauce
4	cups chicken stock
3	cups uncooked white rice
1/4	cup finely chopped flat-leaf parsley
1	pound medium shrimp, peeled and deveined

▸ Rinse the chicken and pat dry with paper towels. Generously season the chicken with salt and pepper. In a large stockpot or Dutch oven over medium-high heat, warm the oil until a few droplets of water sizzle when carefully sprinkled in the pot. Sauté the chicken pieces until browned on all sides, about 5 minutes. Transfer the chicken to a plate. In the same pot, sauté the sausage until browned on all sides, about 5 minutes. Transfer the sausage to the plate with the chicken.

▸ Drain all but about 1 tablespoon of fat from the pot. Add the onion, bell pepper, and celery. Sauté, stirring often, until soft, about 10 minutes. Add the garlic, oregano, thyme, and bay leaves. Sauté until the mixture is cooked down, about 5 minutes more. Season with salt and pepper to taste.

▸ While the vegetable mixture is cooking, combine the tomato sauce and chicken stock in a separate pot. Over high heat, bring to a simmer.

▸ Add the rice to the vegetable mixture, and sauté until translucent, about 3 minutes. Return the meats to the pot and stir to combine. Slowly pour the tomato and stock mixture into the jambalaya, stirring to combine evenly. Stir in the chopped parsley.

▸ Over high heat, bring the jambalaya to a boil. Reduce the heat to medium-low, cover, and simmer until the rice is tender and most of the liquid has been absorbed, about 30 minutes. Turn off the heat and fold in the shrimp. Let stand, covered, until the shrimp are cooked through and the flavors have melded, about 10 minutes. Serve warm.

Serves 6 to 8.

 Variation: Andouille sausage is a smoked, spicy pork sausage that is popular in Cajun recipes such as gumbo and jambalaya. If you can't easily find it in your local grocery, chorizo is an acceptable substitute.

Southwestern Crab Cakes

Corn, jalapeño, and a spicy chipotle sauce give these crab cakes a Southwestern kick.

For the Chipotle Remoulade:

3/4 cup mayonnaise

1/3 cup sour cream

1 can chipotle chile in adobo sauce

1 tablespoon adobo sauce (from the can of chipotle chile in adobo sauce)

Kosher salt and freshly ground pepper

For the Southwestern Crab Cakes:

1 pound jumbo lump crabmeat

1 large egg

1 tablespoon mayonnaise

1 teaspoon Dijon mustard

1/2 teaspoon Worcestershire sauce

2 tablespoons finely chopped fresh cilantro

Kosher salt and freshly ground pepper

1/2 cup fresh or frozen corn kernels

1/2 cup finely diced red bell pepper (about 1 small pepper)

1 tablespoon finely minced fresh jalapeño (about half a jalapeño)

2 tablespoons finely diced shallot (1 shallot)

1/4 cup panko bread crumbs

2 tablespoons vegetable oil

▶ To make the chipotle remoulade: In a food processor puree the mayonnaise, sour cream, chipotle chile, and adobo sauce until smooth. Season with salt and pepper to taste. Cover and refrigerate until ready to serve.

▶ To make the crab cakes: Pick through the crabmeat to remove any extra shell.

▶ In a medium mixing bowl, whisk together the egg, mayonnaise, mustard, Worcestershire sauce, and cilantro. Season with salt and pepper to taste.

▶ Gently fold the crabmeat, corn, red bell pepper, jalapeño, shallots, and bread crumbs into the egg mixture. Shape into 8 crab cakes. Cover with plastic wrap and refrigerate for 1 hour.

▶ In a large cast-iron skillet over medium-high heat, warm the oil until a few droplets of water sizzle in skillet. In batches, so as to not overcrowd the skillet, cook the crab cakes until golden brown on both sides, about 5 minutes per side. Serve the crab cakes with a generous spoonful of the chipotle remoulade. Serve immediately.

Serves 4.

 Cooking Tips: I like to be able to savor the crab in my crab cakes rather than taste a lot of spices or breading. Since this recipe uses just enough fillings to bind the crabmeat, it is imperative that you let the crab cakes set up in the refrigerator for at least an hour before cooking.

This crab cake recipe can also be cooked in the oven. Place the crab cakes on a lightly oiled baking sheet. Place under a preheated broiler, 4 to 6 inches away from the heat source, until golden brown, turning to cook evenly, about 4 to 5 minutes on each side. Watch the crab cakes carefully when broiling to avoid burning them.

 Do Ahead: Crab cakes can be formed and refrigerated for up to 24 hours in advance.

 Freezes Well: Freeze uncooked crab cakes on a sheet tray; then wrap the frozen crab cakes individually in plastic wrap before placing in a resealable freezer bag. Freezing the crab cakes separately allows you to defrost as few or as many as you need.

PASTA & NOODLES

Opposite page: Italian Sausage and Spinach Lasagna (page 106)

Baked Rigatoni with Sausage Meatballs and Spinach

This is my go-to dish for potluck dinners. It is always a hit . . . even with the kids!

1	tablespoon olive oil
1/2	cup finely diced yellow onion (1 small onion)
1/4	cup vodka
1	can (15-ounce) tomato sauce
1	can (28-ounce) whole tomatoes with juice
1 1/2	cups heavy cream
1	teaspoon dried oregano
1	teaspoon dried thyme

Kosher salt and freshly ground black pepper
1	pound sweet Italian sausage, casings removed, sliced 1/4-inch thick
1	box (1 pound/16-ounce) rigatoni, cooked per package directions
1	cup fresh baby spinach, coarsely chopped
4	ounces Fontina cheese, cut into 1/2-inch cubes

▸ Preheat the oven to 375 degrees.

▸ In a large saucepan over medium-high heat, warm the oil until a few droplets of water sizzle when carefully sprinkled in the pan. Add the onion and cook until soft, about 5 minutes. Add the vodka and cook until the liquid has almost evaporated, about 2 minutes. Stir in the tomato sauce, tomatoes, cream, oregano, and thyme. Break up the tomatoes with a fork or spoon. Over high heat, bring to a boil. Season with salt and pepper to taste. Reduce the heat to medium and simmer until thickened, about 30 minutes.

▸ While the sauce is cooking, roll the sausage meat into 1-inch balls. In another large skillet over medium-high heat, sauté the sausage meatballs until well browned, about 8 to 10 minutes. Add the meatballs to the sauce and cook until they are no longer pink in the middle.

▸ In a large mixing bowl, combine the rigatoni, tomato sauce, and spinach leaves. Toss until well combined.

▸ Transfer the mixture to a 9- x 13-inch casserole dish and top with the cheese. Bake until the mixture is slightly browned and bubbling, about 30 minutes.

Serves 8.

 Freezes Well: You can't freeze this dish whole, but you can make an extra batch of the sauce and prepare extra meatballs to store in your freezer for the next time.

 Time-Saving Tip: If you don't have time to make your own sauce, you can substitute a jarred vodka tomato sauce from your local market.

 Back-to-the-Basics: If you have picky eaters in your house who do not eat anything green, just omit the spinach or add it to just half of the dish.

Bow-tie Pasta with Peas and Prosciutto

This is a quick and easy "sauceless" pasta dish that is delicious all year.

2   tablespoons olive oil, divided
2   ounces prosciutto, thinly sliced and cut into
      1/4-inch strips
2   shallots, peeled and thinly sliced into rounds
1   clove garlic, minced
3   cups frozen peas, thawed

Kosher salt and freshly ground black pepper
8   ounces bow-tie pasta, cooked per package
      directions and kept warm
1   tablespoon finely grated lemon zest
1   cup whole milk or part-skim ricotta cheese

▸ Over medium-high heat, warm 1 tablespoon of the oil in a large skillet until a few droplets of water sizzle when carefully sprinkled in the skillet. Add the prosciutto and sauté until crispy. Remove with a slotted spoon and transfer to a paper towel–lined plate to drain. Reserve.

▸ In the same skillet, warm the remaining oil over medium-high heat. Add the shallots and garlic and sauté until soft, about 3 minutes. Add the peas and sauté until heated through, about 5 minutes. Season with salt and pepper to taste. Remove from the heat.

▸ In a large bowl, toss together the warm pasta, pea mixture, prosciutto, lemon zest, and spoonfuls of the ricotta. Serve immediately.

Serves 4.

 Variation: The sautéed peas and prosciutto (without the pasta and ricotta) makes a quick and easy side dish on its own.

Chicken Tetrazzini

This baked pasta dish is a great way to feed a crowd. I often use chicken for this dish, but during the holidays, I like to use leftover turkey.

4 tablespoons unsalted butter, divided, plus extra for the casserole dish and the topping
1 cup grated Parmesan cheese
1/4 cup Italian-style bread crumbs
1 tablespoon olive oil
8 ounces button mushrooms, cleaned, trimmed, and thinly sliced
1/2 cup finely diced yellow onion (about 1 small onion)
4 cloves garlic, minced
1/2 teaspoon dried thyme
1/2 cup dry white wine

2 cups shredded cooked chicken
1 box (16-ounce) linguine, cooked per package directions
1 cup frozen peas, thawed
1/4 cup finely chopped fresh flat-leaf parsley leaves, divided
1/3 cup all-purpose flour
3 cups milk
2 cups heavy cream
1 cup chicken stock
Kosher salt and freshly ground black pepper

▶ Preheat the oven to 425 degrees. Lightly grease a 9- x 13-inch baking dish with butter and set aside.

▶ In a small bowl combine the Parmesan and bread crumbs. Set aside.

▶ In a large saucepan over medium-high heat, melt 1 tablespoon of the butter and the oil. Add the mushrooms and cook, stirring frequently, until the liquid from the mushrooms evaporates and they become slightly golden, about 10 minutes. Add the onion, garlic, and thyme. Cook until the vegetables are soft, about 5 minutes. Add the wine and cook until the liquid has almost evaporated, about 2 minutes. Transfer the mixture to a large bowl. Add the shredded chicken, cooked linguine, peas, and 2 tablespoons of the parsley and set aside.

▶ In the same pan used for the mushrooms, melt the remaining 3 tablespoons of butter over medium-low heat. When the butter starts to foam, add the flour and cook, whisking, until thickened, about one minute. While continuing to whisk, gradually add the milk, heavy cream, and chicken stock. Over medium-high heat, bring the mixture to a boil. Reduce the heat to medium-low and simmer, whisking constantly, until the mixture thickens, about 5 to 8 minutes. Pour the sauce over the pasta mixture, and toss until well combined. Season with salt and pepper to taste.

▶ Transfer the mixture to the prepared baking dish. Sprinkle the bread crumb mixture and the remaining 2 tablespoons of parsley evenly over the pasta. Top with thinly sliced pats of butter. Bake until golden brown, about 30 minutes.

Serves 6 to 8.

Back-to-the-Basics: Do your kids snub anything that has green in it? If so, omit the peas and parsley for a more kid-friendly version.

 Freezes Well.

Mac'n'Cheese with a Twist

Unlike the orangey-yellow boxed variety that many of us grew up on, homemade mac'n'cheese is an ooey, gooey, creamy delight for both the kids and grown-ups at the table.

4 tablespoons unsalted butter, divided, plus extra to grease the casserole dish
2 cups milk
1/4 cup all-purpose flour
1/4 teaspoon freshly grated nutmeg
2 1/2 cups grated white cheddar cheese, divided
1 cup grated Gruyère cheese, divided
Kosher salt and freshly ground black pepper

1/2 pound macaroni, cooked per package directions
1/4 pound country ham, finely diced and lightly browned on both sides
1 teaspoon fresh thyme leaves
1 teaspoon minced fresh flat-leaf parsley
3 thick slices crusty French bread, minced to bread crumbs (about 3/4 cup)

▶ Preheat the oven to 375 degrees. Lightly grease a 2 1/2-quart casserole dish with butter and set aside.

▶ In a small saucepan over medium-high heat, bring the milk just to a boil, then quickly remove from the heat, and set aside.

▶ In a medium saucepan over medium-low heat, melt 3 tablespoons of the butter. When the butter starts to foam, add the flour. Cook, whisking, until thickened, about 1 minute. While continuing to whisk, gradually add the milk. Over medium-high heat, bring the mixture to a boil. Reduce the heat to medium-low and simmer, whisking constantly, until the mixture thickens, about 5 to 8 minutes. Remove the pan from the heat.

▶ Stir in the nutmeg, 2 cups of the cheddar cheese, and 1/2 cup of the Gruyère cheese. Season with salt and pepper to taste. Pour the macaroni into the cheese sauce and stir until well coated. Add the diced ham, thyme, and parsley, and stir until well combined. Place the mixture in the casserole dish.

▶ Melt the remaining 1 tablespoon butter. In a small bowl combine the bread crumbs, the remaining 1/2 cup of cheddar cheese, the remaining 1/2 cup of Gruyère cheese, and the melted butter. Spread the bread crumb mixture evenly over the top of the casserole.

▶ Bake until golden brown, about 40 minutes. Serve warm.

Serves 6.

Cooking Tip: I just love the nutty flavor of Gruyère. Great for melting, this firm cow's milk cheese hails from Switzerland and is now found in most grocery stores. If you can't find it at your grocery store, freshly grated Swiss cheese is an acceptable substitute.

Back-to-the-Basics: Prefer plain old mac'n'cheese? No problem. Omit the herbs and country ham.

Time-Saving Tip: I love the texture of freshly made bread crumbs, but panko bread crumbs are an acceptable "shortcut" substitute.

Pasta Carbonara

In my hometown of Memphis, Nick Vergos is known for his barbecue ribs. His family owns and operates the world-famous Rendezvous restaurant that put Memphis-style dry ribs on the map. Ribs aside, Nick has a lot more culinary tricks up his sleeve. This interpretation of pasta carbonara is one of the many delicious nonbarbecue dishes Nick just whipped up!

For the Gremolata:

- 1/2 cup fresh flat-leaf parsley leaves
- 1/2 teaspoon freshly grated lemon zest
- 1   clove garlic, minced
- 1/4 teaspoon freshly squeezed lemon juice
- 1   teaspoon olive oil
- Pinch of Kosher salt

For the Pasta:

- 1/4 cup plus 1 tablespoon olive oil, divided
- 2   ounces finely chopped pancetta (or tasso ham) (about 1/2 cup)
- 1   box (1 pound/16-ounce) spaghetti
- 3   large eggs
- 1/2 cup finely grated Parmesan cheese, divided
- Kosher salt and freshly grated black pepper
- Pinch of crushed red pepper flakes (optional)

▶ To make the gremolata: In the bowl of a food processor, place the parsley, lemon zest, garlic, lemon juice, olive oil, and a pinch of salt. Coarsely chop until well combined, about 5 to 6 pulses. Set aside. (If you do not have a food processor, you can coarsely chop the parsley and mix the ingredients together in a small bowl.)

▶ To make the pasta: In a small saucepan over medium-high heat, warm 1 tablespoon of the olive oil until a few droplets of water sizzle when carefully sprinkled in the pan. Add the pancetta and cook until crispy and lightly browned, about 4 minutes. Using a slotted spoon, transfer the pancetta to a paper towel–lined plate to drain. Reserve.

▶ Bring a large pot of salted water to a boil. Cook the spaghetti according to package directions. Reserve 1 cup of the cooking liquid and drain the pasta. Keep warm.

▶ In a large mixing bowl crack the eggs and discard the shells. Add 1/4 cup of the Parmesan, 2 tablespoons of the gremolata, and the remaining 1/4 cup olive oil. Stir with a fork to just combine the ingredients; do not emulsify. Season with salt and pepper to taste. Add the hot pasta to the egg mixture, and toss for 3 to 4 minutes to coat the pasta. The sauce should be creamy. If the sauce is too thick, add a little of the reserved pasta water, one teaspoon at a time, to desired consistency. Toss in the pancetta. Add the red pepper flakes to taste, if desired. Adjust the seasonings as needed. Garnish with the remaining Parmesan and additional gremolata to taste. Serve immediately.

Serves 6 to 8.

 Cooking Tip: Nervous about raw eggs? No need to be. The heat of the pasta cooks the eggs into a rich, creamy sauce.

Italian Sausage and Spinach Lasagna

What's not to love about a cheesy lasagna?

For the Sauce:

1	tablespoon olive oil
1/2	pound ground beef
1/2	pound Italian sausage, casings removed
1/2	cup finely diced yellow onion (1 small onion)
1	clove garlic, minced
1	can (28-ounce) crushed tomatoes with juice
1	can (14.5-ounce) diced tomatoes with juice
1	teaspoon dried basil
1	teaspoon dried oregano

Kosher salt and freshly ground black pepper

For the Lasagna:

1	container (15-ounce) whole milk or part-skim ricotta cheese
1 1/2	cups grated Parmesan cheese, divided
1	large egg, lightly beaten

Kosher salt and freshly ground black pepper

9	lasagna noodles, cooked per package directions
1	package (10-ounce) frozen chopped spinach, thawed and drained
3	cups shredded mozzarella cheese

▶ To make the sauce: In a large stockpot over medium-high heat, warm the oil until a few droplets of water sizzle when carefully sprinkled in the pot. Add the beef and sausage and cook, breaking up the meat with a wooden spoon, until the meat is browned and cooked through, about 8 minutes. Transfer the meat to a colander and drain off the excess fat.

▶ Drain all but about 1 tablespoon of fat from the pot. Add the onion and garlic. Reduce the heat to medium and cook, stirring occasionally, until soft, about 4 minutes. Stir in the crushed tomatoes, diced tomatoes, basil, and oregano. Season with salt and pepper to taste. Return the meat to the pot and stir to combine. Over high heat, bring the sauce to a boil. Reduce the heat to medium and simmer until thickened, about 10 minutes. Adjust the seasonings as needed. Reserve until ready to assemble the lasagna.

▶ To assemble the lasagna: Preheat the oven to 375 degrees.

▶ In a medium mixing bowl stir together the ricotta cheese, 1 cup of the Parmesan, and the egg until well combined. Season with salt and pepper to taste.

▶ Spread 1 cup of the tomato sauce over the bottom of a 9- x 13-inch baking dish. Line 3 noodles in the baking dish to create the first layer. Spoon 8 tablespoons of the ricotta mixture evenly across the noodles. Spread half of the frozen spinach evenly across the ricotta. Spoon 1 1/2 cups of the meat sauce evenly on top. Sprinkle 1 cup of the mozzarella evenly over the sauce. Repeat the layering of the noodles, ricotta, spinach, sauce, and mozzarella. Place the remaining three noodles on top. Spoon the remaining ricotta and tomato sauce over the top in layers. Top with the remaining 1 cup of mozzarella and remaining 1/2 cup of Parmesan. Bake uncovered until golden brown and bubbly, about 40 minutes. Let stand 10 minutes before serving.

Serves 8.

 Cooking Tip: This sauce also makes a delicious meaty pasta sauce. Make a double batch and freeze the extra for another day when you want to make lasagna or spaghetti.

 Back-to-the-Basics: Since I like spinach in my lasagna but my children don't, I only put the spinach in one half. If you prefer, you can omit the spinach entirely.

 Time-Saving Tip: This recipe also will work with "No Boil" lasagna noodles. Just soak them in hot water for 10 minutes before using.

 Freezes Well: Unbaked lasagna can be frozen for up to 2 months. Defrost it in your refrigerator overnight before baking.

See picture on page 94.

Shrimp Alfredo

A decadently creamy Alfredo sauce is probably the quickest and easiest pasta sauce to whip up. Serve it plain over your favorite pasta, or dress it up with sautéed shrimp and mushrooms like I do in this version.

For the Alfredo Sauce:

- 1 cup heavy cream
- 2 tablespoons unsalted butter
- 1 cup freshly grated Parmesan cheese
- 1/4 teaspoon freshly grated nutmeg
- Kosher salt and freshly ground black pepper

For the Pasta:

- 1 tablespoon unsalted butter
- 1 tablespoon olive oil

- 1 cup thinly sliced button mushrooms
- 1/2 cup finely diced yellow onion (1 small onion)
- 1 clove garlic, minced
- 1 pound medium shrimp (30-40 count), peeled and deveined
- 1 box (16-ounce) fettuccine, cooked per package directions and kept warm
- Kosher salt and freshly ground black pepper
- 1/4 cup freshly grated Parmesan cheese (optional)

▶ To make the Alfredo sauce: In a medium saucepot over medium-high heat, bring the heavy cream and butter to a boil. As soon as it boils, stir in the Parmesan cheese and cook until melted. Remove the sauce from the heat and add the nutmeg. Season with salt and pepper to taste. Cover and keep warm.

▶ To assemble the pasta: In a large sauté pan over medium-high heat, melt the butter and oil. Add the mushrooms. Cook, stirring frequently, until the liquid from the mushrooms evaporates and they become slightly golden, about 10 minutes. Add the onion and garlic and cook until the vegetables are soft, about 5 minutes. Add the shrimp and sauté until cooked through, about 4 minutes.

▶ In a large mixing bowl toss together the warm pasta, the Alfredo sauce, and the shrimp mixture. Season with salt and pepper to taste. Garnish with Parmesan cheese, if desired. Serve immediately.

Serves 6 to 8.

 Back-to-the-Basics: Not a mushroom fan? Then just omit the mushrooms from this recipe.

Mama's Spaghetti

I wish I could say this recipe came from a true Italian, but this is the name my girls have affectionately given my meaty spaghetti sauce. I always keep a portion or two in my freezer for those days when I run out of time but still want a home-cooked dinner.

1	tablespoon olive oil		1	can (28-ounce) crushed tomatoes with juice
1	pound ground beef		1	teaspoon dried basil leaves
1/2	cup finely diced yellow onion (1 small onion)		1	teaspoon dried thyme
1/2	cup finely diced green bell pepper (1 small pepper)		1	teaspoon dried oregano
1	clove garlic, minced			Kosher salt and freshly ground black pepper
			1	box (16-ounce) spaghetti, cooked per package directions and kept warm

▶ In a large stockpot or Dutch oven over medium-high heat, warm the oil until a few droplets of water sizzle when carefully sprinkled in the pot. Add the meat and cook, breaking up the beef with a wooden spoon, until the meat is browned and cooked through, about 5 minutes. Transfer the cooked meat to a colander and drain off the excess fat.

▶ Drain all but about 1 tablespoon of fat from the pot. Add the onion, bell pepper, and garlic. Reduce the heat to medium and cook, stirring occasionally, until soft, about 4 minutes. Stir in the tomatoes, basil, thyme, and oregano. Season with salt and pepper to taste. Return the meat to the pot and stir to combine. Over high heat, bring the sauce to a boil. Reduce the heat to medium-low and simmer, covered, until thickened, about 45 minutes. Adjust the seasonings as needed. Serve hot over warm pasta.

Serves 6.

 Cooking Tip: Draining the excess fat once the ground beef is cooked makes for a healthier and less greasy finished dish.

 Freezes Well.

Spinach Manicotti

Stuffed with ricotta cheese and spinach, this Italian entree is flavorful and filling. A crispy salad and some fresh Italian bread is all you need to complete this delectable meal.

1   container (15-ounce) whole-milk or part-skim ricotta cheese

1   large egg, lightly beaten

1/2   teaspoon dried thyme

1/2   teaspoon dried oregano

1   cup freshly grated Parmesan cheese, divided

1 1/2 cups shredded mozzarella cheese, divided

1 1/4 cups coarsely chopped fresh spinach or 1 package (10-ounce) frozen chopped spinach, thawed and drained

Kosher salt and freshly ground black pepper

2 1/2 cups Basic Tomato Sauce (see page 230 for the recipe)

12   manicotti shells, cooked per the package directions and cooled

▶ Preheat the oven to 375 degrees.

▶ In a large mixing bowl whisk together the ricotta, egg, thyme, oregano, 1/2 cup of the Parmesan, 1 cup of the mozzarella cheese, and the spinach. Season with salt and pepper to taste.

▶ Spoon a thin layer of tomato sauce in the bottom of a 9- x 13-inch baking dish. Spoon the ricotta-spinach filling into the manicotti shells (about 3 tablespoons ricotta mixture in each) and place the stuffed shells on top of the tomato sauce.

▶ Spoon about 2 cups of the tomato sauce over the top of the manicotti. Garnish with the remaining 1/2 cup of Parmesan cheese and remaining 1/2 cup of mozzarella cheese. Bake until bubbly, about 35 to 40 minutes. Serve immediately.

Serves 6.

 Cooking Tip: Manicotti is so versatile. Using the technique above, you can stuff this fabulous pasta with all of your family's favorite ingredients. Just substitute your favorite meat, cheese, or veggies in place of the spinach.

 Do Ahead: Manicotti can be assembled and covered with the sauce the night before. Store tightly covered in the refrigerator.

 Freezes Well.

Vongole Clam Sauce

Vongole is the Italian name for clams, as well as a delicious pasta dish. I love the flavor of fresh clams, but they are difficult to find at my local market. This quick and easy version uses easy-to-find canned clam sauce instead.

3 tablespoons olive oil
2 cloves garlic, minced
1/4 cup finely chopped fresh flat-leaf parsley
1 can (28-ounce) crushed tomatoes with juice
1 can (10½-ounce) white clam sauce

1/2 teaspoon crushed red pepper flakes
Kosher salt and freshly ground black pepper
1 box (16-ounce) linguine, cooked per the package directions and kept warm

▸ In a large saucepan over medium-high heat, warm the oil until a few droplets of water sizzle when carefully sprinkled in the pan. Add the garlic and parsley, and sauté until fragrant but not browned, about 2 minutes. Add the tomatoes, white clam sauce, and red pepper flakes. Season with salt and pepper to taste. Over high heat, bring to a boil. Reduce the heat to medium-low, cover, and simmer until thickened, about 30 minutes.

▸ Pour the sauce over the warm spaghetti and toss. Serve hot.

Serves 6 to 8.

 Cooking Tip: If you cannot find canned white clam sauce, you can substitute one can (7½-ounce) of minced baby clams. Both work just as well; I just like the extra flavoring that comes from the canned clam sauce.

 Freezes Well.

MELTY SANDWICHES, QUESADILLAS & PIZZAS

Opposite page: Meatball Sub (page 128)

Chicken, Caramelized Onion, and Apple Pizza

There is something about a pizza that I can't resist. I like to get creative with my toppings; caramelized onions and apples are tops on my list.

Unbaked pizza dough, enough for 2 10-inch pizzas, divided into 2 equal dough balls (see page 232 for the recipe)

2 tablespoons olive oil, plus extra to brush on the pizza crust

1 cup thinly sliced yellow onion (about 1 large onion)

1/4 teaspoon dried thyme

Kosher salt and freshly ground pepper

1 1/2 cups shredded mozzarella cheese

1 cup shredded cooked chicken

2 Granny Smith apples, cored and thinly sliced

▸ Preheat the oven to 500 degrees.

▸ Let the pizza dough come to room temperature.

▸ In a large saucepan over medium heat, warm 2 tablespoons of the oil until a few droplets of water sizzle when carefully sprinkled in the pan. Add the onion and thyme. Cook, stirring often, until soft and caramel colored, about 20 to 30 minutes. Season with salt and pepper to taste. Remove from the heat.

▸ Place each dough ball onto a baking sheet. Using your hands, gently flatten, and pull into circles about 10 inches in diameter. Brush each crust with olive oil and season with salt and pepper to taste. Sprinkle the cheese evenly across both crusts. Evenly spread the chicken, onions, and apples across the pizzas. Bake until the crust is golden brown and the toppings are hot, about 10 to 12 minutes.

Serves 4.

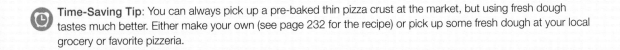

Time-Saving Tip: You can always pick up a pre-baked thin pizza crust at the market, but using fresh dough tastes much better. Either make your own (see page 232 for the recipe) or pick up some fresh dough at your local grocery or favorite pizzeria.

Chicken, Roasted Poblano, and Corn Quesadillas

A quesadilla is simply a toasted tortilla sandwich with melted cheese inside. You can add practically any ingredient to a quesadilla. Here's one of my favorite combinations, but feel free to make your own signature version.

1 large poblano pepper	1 cup shredded cooked chicken
Olive oil for oiling the pan	1 cup frozen corn kernels, thawed
8 fajita-size (6-inch) flour tortillas	
1 cup shredded Monterey Jack cheese	

▶ To roast the poblano pepper, turn the gas burner, or grill, to high heat. Place the pepper flat on the grate and cook until that side is well charred. Rotate the pepper a quarter turn and repeat until each side is well charred. Place the charred, hot pepper in a resealable bag, seal, and steam it until the pepper has cooled to room temperature, about 15 minutes. Remove the pepper from the bag and, using a paper towel, peel off the skin. Gently pull the pepper apart. Remove and discard all the seeds and the stem. Thinly slice the pepper.

▶ Preheat the oven to 200 degrees.

▶ Lightly oil a cast-iron skillet or griddle with olive oil.

▶ Heat the skillet or griddle over medium-high heat. Place 1 tortilla on the hot surface. Evenly sprinkle with 1/4 cup of the cheese, 1/4 cup of the shredded chicken, 1/4 cup of the corn, and 1/4 of the sliced peppers. Cover with another tortilla. Cook until golden brown on the bottom and the cheese has started to melt, about 2 to 3 minutes. Using a flat spatula, carefully turn the quesadilla over and cook until the other side is lightly browned, about 1 to 2 minutes. Transfer the quesadilla to a baking sheet and place in the oven to keep warm. Repeat the process to make the remaining quesadillas, adding more oil to the pan if necessary. Cut the quesadillas into wedges and serve warm.

Serves 4.

 Cooking Tip: If you don't have a cast-iron skillet, just use a stainless steel or nonstick skillet.

There is no need to rinse the peppers in water after they are charred. The blackened bits add a smoky flavor to the dish.

Croque Monsieur

The French have mastered the art of melted cheese sandwiches with their Croque Monsieur. This yummy ham and Gruyère treat is slathered with a béchamel sauce to make it even more indulgent.

2	tablespoons unsalted butter
2	tablespoons all-purpose flour
1	cup milk

Pinch of freshly grated nutmeg
1/4 cup freshly grated Parmesan cheese
2 1/2 cups grated Gruyère cheese, divided
Kosher salt and freshly ground black pepper

8 slices white sandwich bread, lightly toasted
1/4 cup Dijon mustard
1/2 pound baked ham, thinly sliced

▸ Preheat the oven to 450 degrees.

▸ In a small saucepan over low heat, melt the butter. When the butter starts to foam, add the flour. Cook, whisking until thickened, about 1 minute. While continuing to whisk, gradually add the milk. Cook, whisking constantly, until the sauce is thickened, about 2 to 4 minutes. Remove the mixture from the heat and add the nutmeg, Parmesan, and 1/4 cup of the Gruyère. Season with salt and pepper to taste. Set aside.

▸ To assemble the sandwiches, place 4 slices of the toasted bread on a baking sheet. Lightly brush each of the slices with 1 tablespoon of mustard. Top each with one-fourth of the ham and one-eighth of the remaining Gruyère (about 1/4 cup). Top each with one of the remaining toasted bread slices. Pour the cheese sauce evenly over the tops of the sandwiches and sprinkle each with one-fourth of the remaining Gruyère. Transfer to the oven and bake until warmed through, about 5 minutes. Turn on the broiler and broil until the topping is bubbly and lightly browned, about 3 to 5 minutes. Serve hot.

Serves 4.

 Variation: Feeling indulgent? Top your Croque Monsieur with a fried egg and you will be enjoying a treat the French call a Croque Madame.

123

Cuban

You don't have to head to Miami to enjoy this Cuban favorite. It's easy to make this popular pressed sandwich at home.

1   1-pound loaf of ciabatta bread, ends
    trimmed, and cut into 4 pieces
4   tablespoons prepared yellow mustard
4   teaspoons unsalted butter

8   slices Swiss cheese
1/2   pound thinly sliced baked ham
8   ounces roast pork, sliced
1/2   cup sliced dill pickles

▶ Cut the bread in half lengthwise and place on a work surface. To assemble the sandwiches, evenly spread the insides of each sandwich with 1 tablespoon of the mustard and lightly butter the outside of each sandwich with 1 teaspoon of the butter. Inside each sandwich, layer 2 slices of the cheese, one-fourth of the ham, one-fourth of the pork, and one-fourth of the pickles. Close the sandwiches.

▶ Heat your panini maker or sandwich press to medium-high. Place the sandwiches inside, press down, and grill until the cheese is melted and the bread is toasted, about 8 minutes. Serve warm.

Serves 4.

 Cooking Tip: If you don't have a panini press, you can cook the sandwiches on a griddle or skillet. To create the "pressed" sandwich, place a heavy skillet on top of the sandwich and press down as it cooks.

 Variation: Ciabatta bread is an Italian white sandwich bread. If you can't find it at the bakery, use crusty sandwich rolls instead.

Grilled Jalapeño Pimento Cheese Sandwich

There is no better comfort food than warm melted cheese oozing between two slices of crisp buttered bread . . . that is unless you make it ultra-indulgent by using pimento cheese!

For the Jalapeño Pimento Cheese:

- ½ cup cream cheese (4 ounces), at room temperature
- ½ cup mayonnaise
- ½ teaspoon granulated sugar
- 3 cups grated sharp cheddar cheese
- ½ cup finely diced roasted red peppers (1 pepper)
- 2 tablespoons seeded and finely diced fresh jalapeños

Kosher salt and freshly ground black pepper
Dash of hot sauce (optional)

For the Sandwich:

- 8 slices white bread
- 8 teaspoons unsalted butter, softened

▶ To make the pimento cheese: In a large mixing bowl, stir together the cream cheese, mayonnaise, and sugar until smooth. Add the cheddar cheese, red peppers, and the jalapeños. Stir, mashing with a fork, until well combined and relatively smooth. Season with salt and pepper to taste. Add a dash of hot sauce if desired. Cover and refrigerate until ready to use.

▶ To assemble the sandwich: Evenly butter one side of each slice of bread. Place 4 slices, buttered side down, on a work surface. On each slice, evenly spread ½ cup of the pimento cheese. Top each sandwich half with 1 of the remaining buttered slices of bread, buttered side up.

▶ Preheat a griddle (or a large skillet) over medium heat. Place the sandwiches on the warm griddle and cook until the bottom is golden brown, about 4 minutes. Using a flat spatula, carefully turn the sandwiches over. Cook until the second side is golden brown, about 4 minutes.

Serves 4.

Time-Saving Tip: I prefer the texture of the pimento cheese better when I grate the cheddar cheese myself. But if you are in a hurry, you can use packaged grated cheese.

Cooking Tips: This recipe makes approximately 3½ cups of pimento cheese. Pimento cheese will keep for up to 4 days in your refrigerator. (That is, if it lasts that long!)

Back-to-the-Basics: I love the kick that the jalapeños give to this pimento cheese. But if you prefer a milder version, omit the jalapeños.

Meatball Sub

I am so happy my little sister met Craig Monzio in business school. Before their friendship, she couldn't even boil water. Thanks to his lessons, Laura has mastered many of his delicious recipes . . . like these super-tasty meatballs.

For the Meatballs:

- 1/4 cup panko bread crumbs
- 1/4 cup milk
- 1/2 pound ground beef
- 1/4 pound ground pork
- 1/4 pound Italian sausage (mild or hot, depending on your preference), casings removed and crumbled
- 2 tablespoons finely diced shallots
- 5 cloves garlic, minced
- 1/4 cup whole-milk or part-skim ricotta cheese
- 1 cup finely grated Parmesan cheese
- 1 large egg, lightly beaten
- 2 tablespoons chopped fresh flat-leaf parsley
- 1/4 teaspoon freshly grated nutmeg
- 1 teaspoon dried thyme
- 1/2 teaspoon dried oregano
- Kosher salt and freshly ground black pepper

For the sandwiches:

- 2 cups Basic Tomato Sauce (see page 230 for the recipe)
- 4 crusty sandwich rolls
- 2 cups shredded mozzarella cheese

▶ To prepare the meatballs: Preheat the oven to 395 degrees.

▶ In a large mixing bowl combine the bread crumbs and milk until all the milk has been absorbed. Add the ground beef, ground pork, sausage, shallots, garlic, ricotta cheese, Parmesan cheese, egg, parsley, nutmeg, thyme, and oregano. Season with salt and pepper to taste. Gently mix together, by hand or with a fork, until well combined. Shape the mixture into 16 meatballs.

▶ In a large skillet over medium-high heat, warm the oil until a few droplets of water sizzle when carefully sprinkled in the skillet. Working in batches so as to not overcrowd the skillet, cook the meatballs until well-browned on all sides, about 4 to 5 minutes.

Transfer the browned meatballs to a rimmed baking sheet. Once all the meatballs are browned, transfer them to the oven until cooked through and no longer pink in the middle, about 8 to 10 minutes.

▶ To assemble the sandwich: In a medium saucepan over medium heat, warm 2 cups of the sauce. Add the meatballs and toss until well coated and warmed through. Place the sandwich rolls on a baking sheet. Place 4 meatballs on each roll and spoon about 1/2 cup of sauce over the top. Evenly sprinkle the mozzarella cheese over the meatballs. Bake until the cheese has melted and the bread has lightly toasted, about 3 to 5 minutes. Serve warm.

Serves 4.

Do Ahead: The meatballs can be assembled and cooked the night before. Reheat in the sauce before serving.

 Time-Saving Tip: You can substitute store-bought marinara for the homemade tomato sauce.

 Freezes Well: The meatballs freeze well both raw and cooked. Freeze the meatballs on a sheet tray before plac-ing in a resealable freezer bag. Freezing the meatballs separately prevents them from sticking together and allows you to defrost as few or as many as you need.

See picture on page 116.

Reuben

Piled high with corned beef, tangy sauerkraut, and creamy Thousand Island dressing, this warm sandwich is just as tasty at home as at your local deli.

For the Thousand Island Dressing:

- 1/2 cup mayonnaise
- 2 tablespoons sweet pickle relish
- 1/2 teaspoon Worcestershire sauce
- 2 tablespoons chili sauce
- 1 teaspoon freshly squeezed lemon juice
- Kosher salt and freshly ground pepper
- Dash of hot sauce (optional)

For the Sandwiches:

- 8 slices rye bread
- 8 teaspoons unsalted butter
- 3/4 pound thinly sliced cooked corned beef
- 1 cup refrigerated sauerkraut, drained
- 4 slices Swiss cheese

▶ To make the dressing: In a small bowl whisk together the mayonnaise, relish, Worcestershire sauce, chili sauce, and lemon juice until well combined. Season with salt and pepper to taste. Season with the hot sauce, if desired. Cover and refrigerate until ready to use.

▶ To assemble the sandwiches: Evenly butter one side of each slice of bread. Place 4 slices, buttered side down, on a work surface. On each slice, spread 1 tablespoon of the Thousand Island dressing. Layer each sandwich with 1/4 of the corned beef, one-fourth cup of the sauerkraut, and 1 slice of the Swiss cheese. Top each sandwich with 1 of the remaining slices of bread, buttered side up.

▶ Preheat a griddle (or a large skillet) over medium heat. Place the sandwiches on the warm griddle and cook until the bottom is golden brown, about 4 minutes. Using a flat spatula, carefully turn the sandwiches over. Cook until the second side is golden brown, about 4 minutes. Serve hot, with a side of extra Thousand Island dressing if desired.

Serves 4.

 Cooking Tip: Cook the sandwiches slowly in order to allow the cheese to melt without burning the bread. If the outside is browning too quickly, reduce the heat, cover, and cook slowly until the cheese melts.

 Do Ahead: The Thousand Island dressing will last up to 4 days covered and refrigerated.

 Time-Saving Tip: You can always use a bottled Thousand Island dressing if preferred.

Sausage & Roasted Bell Pepper Calzone

A calzone is a folded pizza with all the toppings inside the crust. Serve your favorite tomato sauce on the side for dipping.

Unbaked pizza dough, enough for 2 10-inch
    pizzas, divided into 4 equal dough balls (see
    page 232 for the recipe)
1   tablespoon olive oil, plus extra to brush on
    the crust
3/4 pound mild or hot Italian sausage, casings
    removed
1   cup thinly sliced red onion (1 large onion)
Kosher salt and freshly ground black pepper

3/4 cup whole-milk or part-skim ricotta cheese
1 1/2 cups shredded mozzarella cheese
3/4 cup grated Parmesan cheese
1   large egg, lightly beaten
2   teaspoons dried oregano
1   teaspoon crushed red pepper flakes
1/2 cup finely diced roasted red bell pepper

▶ Preheat the oven to 450 degrees.

▶ Let the pizza dough come to room temperature.

▶ In a large saucepan over medium heat, warm the oil until a few droplets of water sizzle when carefully sprinkled in the pan. Add the sausage and cook, breaking up the meat with a wooden spoon, until the meat is browned and cooked through, about 5 minutes. Transfer the meat to a colander and drain off the excess fat.

▶ Drain off all but about 1 tablespoon of fat from the pan. Add the sliced onion and cook, stirring often, until soft and slightly caramelized, about 10 minutes. Season with salt and pepper to taste. Remove the onions from the heat.

▶ In a large mixing bowl combine the ricotta, mozzarella, Parmesan, egg, oregano, and red pepper flakes. Fold in the cooked sausage, cooked onions, and roasted red bell pepper. Season with salt and pepper to taste.

▶ Place each dough ball onto a baking sheet. Using your hands, gently flatten and pull into circles, about 5 inches in diameter. Brush each crust with olive oil and season the dough with salt and pepper to taste. Spoon one-fourth of the filling on half of each of the discs, leaving a 1-inch border. Fold the other side over the filling to make a half-moon shape and pinch the edges together, making sure the calzone is completely sealed. Repeat with the remaining calzones. Brush the tops with olive oil.

▶ Using a fork, poke a few holes in the top for steam to release. Bake until the crust is golden brown, about 20 to 25 minutes. Serve hot.

Serves 4.

 Variation: The cheese and egg mixture is the basic calzone filling base. You can substitute your favorite ingredients for the sausage, onion, and roasted peppers. Try spinach and mushrooms for a vegetarian version. Add pepperoni and salami for a meat lover's treat.

Sloppy Joes

What can be more fun to eat than a sandwich that is messy by design? This flavorful homemade version will make this meaty dish a favorite casual supper.

1	tablespoon vegetable oil
1/2	cup finely diced yellow onion (1 small onion)
1/2	cup seeded and finely diced green bell pepper (1 pepper)
1	pound ground beef
1	can (16-ounce) red kidney beans, drained and rinsed
2	tablespoons tomato paste
1	cup tomato sauce
2	tablespoons cider vinegar
1/4	teaspoon ground cinnamon
1/2	teaspoon firmly packed light brown sugar
	Kosher salt and freshly ground black pepper
4	hamburger buns, split

▶ In a large stockpot over medium-high heat, warm the oil until a few droplets of water sizzle when carefully sprinkled in the pot. Add the onion and green bell pepper. Cook, stirring occasionally, until the vegetables are soft, about 4 minutes. Add the meat and cook, breaking up the beef with a wooden spoon, until the meat is browned and cooked through, about 8 minutes.

Stir in the beans, tomato paste, tomato sauce, cider vinegar, cinnamon, and brown sugar. Season with salt and pepper to taste. Reduce the heat to medium and simmer, stirring frequently, until the flavors have blended, about 15 minutes.

▶ To serve, toast the buns. Divide the mixture evenly between the 4 buns and serve immediately.

Serves 4.

 Cooking Tip: For a lower fat Sloppy Joe, use 95% lean ground beef, ground turkey, or ground chicken.

 Back-to-the-Basics: If you are not a fan of beans, just omit them for a simply meaty Sloppy Joe.

 Freezes Well.

Tuna Melt

There used to be a sandwich shop around the corner that served the best tuna salad. The owner, Alyce Mantia, once told me that her secret ingredients were lemon and oregano. Hope you enjoy this little twist as much as I do.

2   cans (5-ounce) solid white tuna, drained and flaked
1/4   cup thinly sliced celery (about 1 rib)
1   tablespoon finely diced yellow onion
1   tablespoon finely grated lemon zest
1   tablespoon freshly squeezed lemon juice
1/4   cup mayonnaise

1/4   teaspoon dried oregano
Kosher salt and freshly ground black pepper
4   slices crusty white or sourdough bread, lightly toasted
8   slices of tomato
4   slices cheddar cheese

▸ Preheat the broiler.

▸ In a medium mixing bowl stir together the tuna, celery, onion, lemon zest, lemon juice, mayonnaise, and oregano until well combined. Season with salt and pepper to taste.

▸ To assemble the sandwich, place the bread slices on a baking sheet. Evenly spread one-fourth of the tuna salad onto each of the slices. Top each sandwich with 2 tomato slices and a slice of cheese. Broil until the cheese is melted, about 3 to 5 minutes. Serve hot.

Serves 4.

 Variation: Mix up the flavor by using either rye bread or split English muffins instead of the traditional white bread. You can also substitute Swiss cheese or Pepper Jack for the cheddar.

 Do Ahead: The tuna salad can be made up to two days in advance. Store covered in the refrigerator.

POTATOES, RICE, GRAINS & STUFFINGS

Almond Rice Pilaf

Tired of plain old white rice? Jazz up this plain-Jane staple by cooking the rice in stock rather than water. I also like the texture the onions and slivered almonds add.

1	tablespoon unsalted butter		1/2	cup slivered almonds
1	tablespoon olive oil		1	cup uncooked long-grain white rice
1/4	cup finely diced yellow onion (1/2 small onion)		2	cups chicken stock

Kosher salt and freshly ground black pepper

▶ In a medium saucepot, melt the butter and olive oil over medium-high heat. Add the onions and almonds and cook until the onions are soft, about 5 minutes. Stir in the rice and cook until translucent, about 1 minute. Slowly stir in the stock. Season with salt and pepper to taste. Over high heat, bring the mixture to a boil. Reduce the heat to medium-low and simmer, covered, until the rice is tender and the liquid is absorbed, about 15 to 20 minutes. Serve warm.

 Cooking Tip: My favorite rice to use is basmati. It has longer grains than most varieties of rice and tends to be less sticky.

 Variation: You can omit the almonds if you would prefer a nut-free version.

Baked Cheese Grits

Using quick-cooking white grits gives this dish a deliciously creamy texture. For an added kick, add chopped jalapeño peppers.

1/4 cup (1/2 stick) unsalted butter, plus extra to grease the baking dish
41/2 cups water
11/4 cups quick-cooking grits

31/2 cups grated cheddar cheese, divided
Kosher salt and freshly ground black pepper
1   clove garlic, minced
3   large eggs, lightly beaten

▶ Preheat the oven to 350 degrees. Lightly grease a 9- x 13-inch baking dish with butter and set aside.

▶ In a large saucepan over high heat, bring the water to a boil. Stir in the grits and reduce the heat to medium-low. Cover and simmer until thickened, about 5 minutes. Remove the grits from the heat and stir in the butter and 3 cups of the cheese until the cheese has melted, about 1 minute. Season with salt and pepper to taste. Stir in the garlic and eggs until well combined.

▶ Pour the grits into the prepared baking dish. Evenly sprinkle the remaining 1/2 cup of the cheese across the top. Bake, uncovered, until bubbly and lightly browned, about 30 minutes. Serve warm.

Serves 8 to 10.

 Cooking Tip: For a "grittier" texture, you can substitute stone-ground grits. Stone-ground grits take much longer to cook, so be sure to prepare them per the package directions before adding the cheese, butter, and eggs.

Baked Sweet Potato Fries

Oven fries are easy to make and much healthier for you than the deep-fried variety. Sweet potatoes do not crisp up as much as Russet potatoes, but they sure do make a yummy side dish.

5	sweet potatoes	6	sprigs fresh thyme
3	tablespoons olive oil		Kosher salt and freshly ground black pepper

▸ Preheat the oven to 395 degrees.

▸ To make the fries, peel the potatoes and cut each potato into 1/2-inch-thick lengthwise strips.

▸ In a large mixing bowl, toss the potatoes, oil, and thyme. Season with salt and pepper to taste. On a baking sheet, evenly spread the fries in a single layer. Bake until the fries are tender and golden brown, turning occasionally, about 30 to 40 minutes. Serve immediately.

Serves 4 to 6.

 Back-to-the-Basics: The fresh thyme adds a little "sophistication" to these fries. Feel free to omit the herb or to substitute Russet potatoes.

Butternut Squash Risotto

Risotto sounds complicated, but it is actually very easy to make. All it takes is a little patience to wait for the rice to absorb the liquid.

1	medium butternut squash (about 1 pound)	1 1/2 cups Arborio rice	
5	cups chicken stock	1/2 cup dry white wine	
2	tablespoons unsalted butter	1/4 cup finely grated Parmesan cheese	
1	tablespoon olive oil	Kosher salt and freshly ground black pepper	
1/4	cup finely chopped yellow onion (1/2 small onion)		

▶ Peel, halve, and remove the seeds from the squash. Cut it into 1/2-inch pieces. In a medium saucepan place the squash and enough water to cover by 1 inch. Over high heat, bring to a boil. Reduce the heat to medium and simmer until fork-tender, but not too soft, about 8 to 10 minutes. Drain and set aside.

▶ In a medium saucepot over high heat, bring the stock to a boil. Reduce the heat to low.

▶ In a large saucepot over medium heat, melt the butter and oil. Add the onions and cook, stirring, until soft, about 2 to 3 minutes. Add the rice and stir with a wooden spoon, making sure all the grains are coated.

Cook until translucent, about 1 minute. Add the white wine and simmer, uncovered, until the liquid has almost evaporated, about 3 to 5 minutes. Add the simmering stock, 1/2 cup at a time, stirring frequently. Wait until each addition is almost completely absorbed before adding the next 1/2 cup of stock. The risotto is done when the rice is tender, but still firm.

▶ Stir in the cooked squash and the Parmesan cheese. Season with salt and pepper to taste. Cook until the squash is reheated and the cheese is melted, about 2 to 5 minutes. Serve immediately.

Serves 4.

 Cooking Tip: This is the basic recipe for making risotto. Once you have mastered this simple recipe, you can make any flavor combination you are craving.

Cheesy Twice-Baked Potatoes

You can serve twice-baked potatoes as a side dish, but I think this overstuffed version is a meal in itself.

5	large baking potatoes, scrubbed and patted dry
1	cup sour cream
4	tablespoons (1/2 stick) unsalted butter

6	slices bacon, cooked and crumbled
2	tablespoons minced fresh chives
2	cups grated sharp cheddar cheese, divided
	Kosher salt and freshly ground black pepper

▶ Preheat the oven to 400 degrees.

▶ Prick the potatoes all over with the tines of a fork and place them on a large baking sheet. Bake until fork tender, about 1 hour. Set aside until cool enough to handle.

▶ Peel 1 potato, place the flesh in a large mixing bowl, and discard the skin. Slice the top quarter off the remaining potatoes lengthwise. Using a spoon, scoop the flesh from the tops into the bowl and discard the skins. Carefully scoop out the flesh from the potato bottoms, leaving a shell 1/4-inch thick. Place the potato shells on the baking sheet.

▶ Using a potato masher or fork, mash the potato flesh until smooth. Add the sour cream, butter, bacon, chives, and 1 cup of the cheese. Stir until combined. Season with salt and pepper to taste.

▶ Spoon the potato mixture back in to the potato shells, mounding it high, and top with the remaining 1 cup of the cheese. Bake the potatoes until heated through and the cheese is melted, about 20 minutes. Serve hot.

Serves 4.

 Cooking Tip: Feel free to experiment with your fillings. Mix in spinach, chicken, or your favorite cheeses. My sister's mother-in-law even adds canned tuna to hers!

 Do Ahead: Baking the potatoes is the most time-consuming part of this recipe. Bake them up to 24 hours in advance to get a head start on this dish.

 Freezes Well: The assembled twice-baked potatoes freeze well before baking the second time. Tightly wrap in plastic wrap and then a layer of foil. Thaw before baking.

Cornbread and Sausage Stuffing

Cornbread stuffing is a Southern classic. Serve it as a side dish, or make a smaller batch to use as a stuffing for pork chops.

Unsalted butter to grease the baking dish
1   8-inch pan prepared cornbread, cut into
    3/4-inch cubes (about 8 cups)
1   tablespoon olive oil
1   pound country-style fresh pork sausage,
    crumbled

1   cup finely diced yellow onion (about 1 large
    onion)
1   cup finely sliced celery (about 3 ribs)
2   cups chicken stock
3   large eggs
Kosher salt and freshly ground black pepper

▶ Preheat the oven to 350 degrees. Grease a 9- x 13-inch casserole dish with butter and set aside. Place the cornbread cubes in a large mixing bowl and set aside.

▶ In a large skillet over medium-high heat, warm the oil until a few droplets of water sizzle when carefully sprinkled in the skillet. Add the sausage and cook, breaking up the meat with a wooden spoon, until the meat is browned and cooked through, about 8 minutes. Transfer the cooked meat to a colander and drain off the excess fat. Transfer the drained sausage to the cornbread mixing bowl.

▶ Drain all but about 1 tablespoon of fat from the skillet. Reduce the heat to medium. Add the onion and

celery. Cook, stirring occasionally, until soft, about 4 minutes. Transfer the cooked vegetables to the cornbread mixture. Toss to combine.

▶ In a medium mixing bowl, whisk together the chicken stock and the eggs. Add to the cornbread mixture and toss to evenly coat. Season with salt and pepper to taste.

▶ Transfer the stuffing to the prepared casserole dish. Bake, loosely covered with foil, until set and warmed through, about 30 minutes. Remove the foil and bake until the top is browned, about 15 minutes. Serve warm.

Serves 8 to 10.

 Cooking Tip: You can either make your own cornbread or pick up an already prepared pan at your local market.

 Freezes Well.

Curried Couscous

This could almost be considered a "no-cook" dish since the only cooking is boiling water. The rest is just assembly.

1   box (10-ounce) uncooked couscous
1   cup dried cranberries
1/2 teaspoon curry powder
2   cups water
4   tablespoons olive oil, divided
Kosher salt
1/2 cup pine nuts, toasted
1/2 cup thinly sliced scallions

2   tablespoons finely chopped fresh flat-leaf parsley
1/2 cup freshly squeezed orange juice
1   tablespoon freshly squeezed lemon juice
1   clove garlic, minced
Freshly ground black pepper

▶ In a large mixing bowl combine the couscous, cranberries, and curry powder. In a medium saucepan combine the water, 1 tablespoon of the oil, and a pinch of salt. Over high heat, bring the water mixture to a boil. Pour the boiling water over the couscous, stir, cover tightly, and let stand for 5 minutes. Uncover and fluff the couscous lightly with a fork.

▶ Add the pine nuts, scallions, and parsley, and stir to combine.

▶ In a small bowl whisk together the orange juice, lemon juice, remaining 3 tablespoons of oil, and the garlic. Pour over the couscous mixture and toss to combine. Season with salt and pepper to taste. Serve warm or chilled.

Serves 6.

Cooking Tip: To toast pine nuts, spread the nuts evenly on a baking sheet and place in a preheated 325-degree oven. Toast, stirring occasionally so that the nuts evenly brown, until they start to turn golden and are fragrant, about 3 minutes. Remove from the oven and let cool. Pine nuts can also be toasted in your toaster oven.

Do Ahead: Couscous can be made hours ahead of time. Many prefer to make it in advance and let the flavors meld as it chills in the refrigerator.

Potatoes Au Gratin

This dish looks so elegant on the table that no one will believe how easy it was to make. I often serve it at dinner parties with steaks or roasts.

3 tablespoons unsalted butter, plus extra to grease the baking dish and the foil
1½ cups milk
1 cup heavy cream
2 cloves garlic, minced

⅛ teaspoon freshly grated nutmeg
5 medium baking potatoes
Kosher salt and freshly ground black pepper
¼ cup grated Gruyère cheese

▸ Preheat the oven to 375 degrees. Lightly grease a 9- x 13-inch baking dish with butter and set aside.

▸ In a large saucepot combine the milk, cream, butter, garlic, and nutmeg. Peel the potatoes and cut into slices about ⅛-inch thick. Add the potato slices to the milk mixture to prevent discoloration.

▸ Over medium-high heat, bring the milk mixture to a simmer and cook until the potatoes are slightly tender but still firm, about 5 minutes. Season with salt and pepper to taste. Using a slotted spoon, transfer the potatoes to the prepared baking dish, arranging the top layer of the potatoes in an overlapping pattern, if desired. Pour the milk mixture over the potatoes. Sprinkle the cheese evenly over the top. Cover the dish with a buttered piece of aluminum foil, buttered side down.

▸ Bake until the potatoes are fork tender, about 30 minutes. Remove the foil and bake until the potatoes are golden brown, about 20 minutes.

Serves 6 to 8.

 Cooking Tip: The difference between freshly grated nutmeg and commercially ground is night and day. To grate whole nutmeg, use a special nutmeg grater or scrape the seed over the finest rasps of your box grater. I buy my whole nutmeg at the grocery in a specially designed jar with a grinder built into the lid.

Roasted Garlic Mashed Potatoes

Mashed potatoes are always a favorite, and roasted garlic makes them sublime.

For the Roasted Garlic:

1 head of garlic
1 tablespoon olive oil
Kosher salt and freshly ground black pepper

For the Mashed Potatoes:

3 pounds red potatoes, peeled and cubed
Kosher salt and freshly ground black pepper
1/2 cup heavy cream, warmed
4 tablespoons unsalted butter
1/4 cup olive oil

▶ To roast the garlic: Preheat the oven to 350 degrees. Trim about 1/2-inch off the top of the head of garlic, leaving the head intact. Place the garlic in a small baking dish. Drizzle 1 tablespoon olive oil over the cut top of the garlic. Season with salt and pepper. Cover with aluminum foil and bake until the garlic is soft, about 1 hour. Set aside until cool enough to handle. Squeeze the base of the garlic to pop the cloves from the skin.

▶ To make the mashed potatoes: In a large stockpot place the potatoes, 1 teaspoon of salt, and enough cold water to cover the potatoes by 1 inch. Over high heat, bring to a boil. Reduce the heat to medium-low and simmer until the potatoes are fork tender, about 20 to 25 minutes. Drain the potatoes. While the potatoes are still hot, mash the potatoes through a potato ricer. Place the mashed potatoes back into the cooking pot.

▶ Puree the roasted garlic with the heavy cream in a food processor. Add the garlic puree, butter, and olive oil to the mashed potatoes and stir to combine. Season with salt and pepper to taste. Serve immediately.

Serves 6 to 8.

 Cooking Tip: Using a potato ricer makes for smoother mashed potatoes. For a slightly lumpier mixture, use a potato masher instead. Never use a food processor, because it makes potatoes gluey.

 Time-Saving Tip: Want the garlic flavor, but don't have the time for roasting? Substitute roasted garlic olive oil for the plain olive oil.

 Back-to-the-Basics: Not a garlic fan? Just omit the garlic.

Red Beans and Rice

Red beans and rice is the quintessential Louisianan comfort food. Nothing satisfies like a steaming bowl of tender, flavorful beans over classic white rice.

1	pound dried red kidney beans, rinsed and sorted
1	tablespoon olive oil
1/2	cup finely diced yellow onion (1 small onion)
1/2	cup seeded and finely diced green bell pepper (1 small pepper)
1/4	cup finely sliced celery (about 1 rib)
1	clove garlic, minced
2	tablespoons finely chopped fresh flat-leaf parsley

1	teaspoon dried oregano
1	teaspoon dried thyme
2	bay leaves
Kosher salt and freshly ground black pepper	
1/2	pound smoked ham hock
1/2	pound smoked Andouille sausage, thinly sliced into rounds
10	cups water
6	cups cooked white rice, warm

▶ Place the beans in a large bowl or pot and cover with water by 2 inches. Let soak for 8 hours or overnight. Drain and set aside.

▶ In a large stockpot or Dutch oven, warm the oil until a few droplets of water sizzle when carefully sprinkled in the pot. Add the onion, bell pepper, celery, and garlic, and cook until the vegetables are soft, about 5 minutes. Stir in the parsley, oregano, thyme, and bay leaves. Season with salt and pepper to taste. Add the ham hock and sausage. Cook, stirring, to brown the ham hock and sausage, about 4 minutes. Add the beans and water.

▶ Over high heat, bring the mixture to a boil. Reduce the heat to medium-low, cover, and simmer, stirring occasionally, until the beans are tender, about 1 1/2 hours. Add additional water while cooking if necessary.

▶ Remove the ham hock from the pot and pull the meat from the bones. Discard the bones. Roughly chop the meat and return it to the pot of beans. Adjust seasonings as needed. Discard the bay leaves. Spoon over white rice to serve.

Serves 6.

 Cooking Tip: Add your favorite hot sauce for a little heat.

 Do Ahead: Cooked red beans store very well in the refrigerator. Some even say they taste better the second day!

Sweet Potato Casserole

This dish is just too good to be saved only for the holidays.

6   tablespoons unsalted butter, plus extra to
    grease the baking dish
8   sweet potatoes, scrubbed and patted dry
1   tablespoon ground cinnamon

1/4   cup firmly packed light brown sugar
Kosher salt and freshly ground black pepper
2   cups baby marshmallows

▶ Preheat the oven to 400 degrees. Lightly grease a 2¹/₂-quart baking dish with butter and set aside.

▶ Line a baking sheet with foil or parchment paper. Place the potatoes on the baking sheet and bake until fork tender, about 1 hour. Set aside until cool enough to handle. Reduce the oven temperature to 350 degrees.

▶ Slice the potatoes in half lengthwise and, using a spoon, scoop the flesh into a large mixing bowl.

Discard the skins. Using a potato masher or fork, mash the potato flesh until smooth. Add the butter, cinnamon, and brown sugar. Stir until well combined. Season with salt and pepper to taste.

▶ Spoon and level the mixture into the prepared dish. Evenly top with a single layer of marshmallows. Bake until the marshmallows are puffed and golden and the potatoes are heated through, about 30 minutes.

Serves 6 to 8.

 Do Ahead: This can be made a day ahead, covered, and refrigerated. Return to room temperature before baking.

 Time-Saving Tip: I prefer the flavor of freshly baked sweet potatoes. But if you are short on time, you can boil peeled and cubed sweet potatoes until tender, about 20 minutes, and drain well. Precooked sweet potatoes, which can be found in the grocery freezer section, are another shortcut.

 Variation: My good friend Allison Lemm makes a delicious Bourbon Pecan version of this recipe. Stir 2 tablespoons of bourbon into the sweet potato mixture and add a 1/4 cup of toasted chopped pecans to the marshmallow topping.

Three-Grain Casserole

This delicious grain casserole comes from the kitchen of my good friend Jenny Mallery Vergos. The base recipe is so versatile. Jenny often mixes in carrots, corn, black beans, and Monterey Jack cheese. I like it with greens and goat cheese. Feel free to experiment by adding your favorite cooked vegetables to the grain mixture.

3	tablespoons olive oil
8	ounces button mushrooms, cleaned, trimmed, and thinly sliced
1/2	cup finely diced yellow onion (1 small onion)
1	clove garlic, minced
2 to 3	cups coarsely chopped greens (collards, kale, or mustard), woody stems discarded

1/2	cup uncooked pearl barley
1/4	cup uncooked brown rice
1/4	cup uncooked bulgur
1 1/4	cups vegetable or chicken stock
2	tablespoons soy sauce
1/2	cup crumbled goat cheese

▶ Preheat the oven to 350 degrees.

▶ In a large skillet over medium-high heat, warm the oil until a few droplets of water sizzle when carefully sprinkled in the skillet. Add the mushrooms, onion, garlic, and greens. Cook until the vegetables are soft, about 5 minutes. Stir in the barley, rice, and bulgur and cook for 3 minutes. Transfer the mixture to a 1 1/2-quart baking dish. Add the stock and soy sauce and stir to combine. Cover tightly and bake, stirring halfway through cooking, until the grains are tender, about 1 hour.

▶ Remove the casserole from the oven, uncover, and sprinkle the cheese evenly over the top. Re-cover and let stand until the cheese melts, about 5 minutes. Serve warm.

Serves 6 to 8.

 Cooking Tip: Bulgur is a whole grain that is high in fiber and protein. It is found next to the rices and dried beans in most supermarkets.

Wild Mushroom, Rosemary, and Hazelnut Dressing

This dressing is delicious with turkey and also pairs nicely with red meat.

6	tablespoons unsalted butter, plus extra to grease the baking dish
1	1-pound loaf rosemary bread, cut into 1/2-inch cubes (about 8 cups)
8	ounces button mushrooms, cleaned, trimmed, and thinly sliced (about 2 cups)
3/4	pound fresh shitake mushrooms, stemmed and quartered (about 2 cups)
1/2	cup finely diced yellow onion (1 small onion)

2	cloves garlic, minced
2 1/2	teaspoons dried rosemary
	Kosher salt and freshly ground black pepper
1	cup dry white wine
2	cups hazelnuts, toasted, skins removed, and coarsely chopped
2	cups chicken stock
2	large eggs, lightly beaten

▸ Preheat the oven to 350 degrees. Lightly grease a 9- x 13-inch baking dish with butter and set aside.

▸ Place the bread on a rimmed baking sheet and bake in the middle of the oven until the bread is toasted dry and lightly browned, about 15 minutes. Set aside to cool.

▸ In a large saucepan over medium-high heat, melt 6 tablespoons butter. Add the button mushrooms, shiitake mushrooms, and onion. Cook, stirring occasionally, until soft and lightly browned, about 6 to 8 minutes. Add the garlic and rosemary. Cook, stirring, until fragrant, about 1 minute. Season with salt and pepper to taste. Add the white wine and, over high heat, bring to a boil. Reduce the heat to medium-low and simmer, stirring with a wooden spoon to scrape the brown bits off the bottom of the pan, until the liquid is almost evaporated, about 4 minutes. Transfer the mixture to a large mixing bowl. Add the bread and hazelnuts, and toss to combine.

▸ In a medium mixing bowl, whisk together the stock and eggs. Add to the bread mixture and toss to evenly coat.

▸ Transfer the dressing to the prepared baking dish. Bake, loosely covered with foil, until set and warmed through, about 30 minutes. Remove the foil and bake until the top is browned, about 15 minutes. Serve warm.

Serves 6 to 8.

 Do Ahead: You can toast the bread a day or two ahead and store the cooled croutons in a resealable plastic bag. The hazelnuts can be toasted several days ahead as well. The mushrooms and onions can be cleaned and cut the day ahead and stored separately in the fridge. It is best to assemble all the ingredients the day you plan to serve the dish.

 Cooking Tip: If you cannot find rosemary bread at your local market, substitute a crusty French bread and add an extra teaspoon of dried rosemary.

VEGETABLES

Asparagus with Brown Butter

Brown butter is one of my signature cooking "tricks." I use it to season vegetables, as a sauce for roasted fish, and have even drizzled it into cake batter. The classic French term for this cooking technique is beurre noisette, *which literally translates to "hazelnut butter." By slightly browning the butter, you give it a delicious nutty flavor. Be careful, though; this sauce is ready the moment it starts to brown. If you overcook it, it will taste burnt.*

Kosher salt
1   bunch (about 1 pound) asparagus, tough woody ends snapped off and discarded

3   tablespoons unsalted butter
Freshly ground black pepper

▶ Fill a medium pot with water and add 1 tablespoon of salt. Over high heat, bring the salted water to a boil. Add the asparagus and cook until vibrant green and crisp tender, 1 to 1¹/2 minutes. Drain the asparagus. Set aside.

▶ Wipe the pot dry. Add the butter and over medium-high heat, cook, swirling the pot occasionally, until the butter stops foaming and begins to brown. Remove from the heat. Add the asparagus and toss until well coated. Season with salt and pepper to taste. Serve immediately.

Serves 4.

 Cooking Tip: The ends of asparagus spears tend to be tough and woody. To trim, simply bend each stalk, and it will naturally break off in just the right spot.

 Do Ahead: The process of cooking a vegetable in boiling salted water is called *blanching*. Blanching prevents the vegetable from being overcooked when reheated or, in this case, tossed with the brown butter. You can use this same technique to cook vegetables in advance. When you drain the blanched vegetable, immediately immerse it in an ice-water bath to stop the cooking process. Drain again and refrigerate until ready to serve.

Braised Red Cabbage

This sweet-and-sour side is very colorful and easy to prepare. I like to serve it with roast pork.

2	tablespoons olive oil
8	cups shredded red cabbage (1/2 large head)
1	cup thinly sliced red onion (1 large onion)
2	teaspoons finely grated orange zest
1/4	cup freshly squeezed orange juice
1/2	cup port wine

1/4	cup red wine vinegar
1/4	cup firmly packed light brown sugar
2	tablespoons water

Kosher salt and freshly ground black pepper

▸ In a large stockpot or Dutch oven over medium heat, warm the oil until a few droplets of water sizzle when carefully sprinkled in the pot. Add the cabbage and onion. Cover and cook, stirring occasionally, until the cabbage is wilted, about 12 minutes.

▸ Uncover and add the orange zest, orange juice, port wine, red wine vinegar, brown sugar, and water.

Season with salt and pepper to taste. Over high heat, bring the mixture to a boil. Reduce the heat to medium and cook, stirring occasionally, until the sauce has thickened, about 30 minutes. Adjust the seasonings as necessary and serve warm.

Serves 6.

 Cooking Tips: The cabbage will be very tender, moist, and a dark reddish purple when it is ready. Overcooking will result in cabbage that is dry or mushy.

If you do not keep port in the house, you can substitute a fruity red wine.

Brussels Sprouts and Bacon

Doesn't bacon make everything taste better? My friend Kelly English serves a version of this warm dish as a first-course salad at Restaurant Iris, his popular Memphis restaurant. I dish it up as a hearty side.

1½ pounds Brussels sprouts
Kosher salt
3 slices of bacon, cut into ¼-inch pieces

2 tablespoons unsalted butter
Freshly ground black pepper

▸ Trim the bottoms off of the Brussels sprouts and slice in half.

▸ Fill a large pot with water and add 1 tablespoon of salt. Over high heat, bring the salted water to a boil. Add the sprouts and cook until fork tender, about 7 to 8 minutes. Drain and reserve.

▸ In a large skillet over medium-high heat, cook the bacon until crispy, about 4 minutes. With a slotted spoon, transfer the bacon to a paper towel–lined plate to drain. Reserve.

▸ Pour all but about 1 tablespoon of fat from the skillet. Add the butter and allow it to melt. Add the sprouts and sauté until they are lightly browned, about 5 minutes. Season with salt and pepper to taste. Return the bacon to the pan and toss to combine. Serve warm.

Serves 4.

 Cooking Tip: Regular bacon is fine, but for an extra bacon-y flavor, use thick-cut artisan bacon or Italian pancetta.

 Do Ahead: The Brussels sprouts can be blanched ahead of time and then reheated when sautéed. (See the Do Ahead tip on page 169 for blanching instructions.)

Cauliflower Au Gratin

This dish is served at every Hanemann family get-together. For years it was the only way I would eat cauliflower!

8 tablespoons (1 stick) unsalted butter, plus extra to grease the baking dish and for the topping
Kosher salt
2 large heads cauliflower, green leaves discarded, trimmed, and cut into large individual florets

4 tablespoons all-purpose flour
3 cups milk
3/4 cup grated Gruyère cheese
3/4 cup grated Parmesan cheese
1/4 teaspoon cayenne pepper
Freshly ground black pepper
1 cup plain bread crumbs

▶ Preheat the oven to 325 degrees. Lightly grease a 2½-quart baking dish with butter and set aside.

▶ Fill a large pot with water and add 1 tablespoon of salt. Over high heat, bring the salted water to a boil. Add the cauliflower and cook until fork tender but still firm, about 7 to 8 minutes. Drain and reserve.

▶ In a medium saucepan over medium-low heat, melt the butter. When the butter starts to foam, add the flour and cook, whisking, until thickened, about one minute. While continuing to whisk, gradually add the milk. Over medium-high heat, bring the mixture to a boil. Reduce the heat to medium-low and simmer, whisking constantly, until the mixture thickens, about 5 to 8 minutes. Remove the pan from the heat. Stir in the cheeses. Add the cayenne pepper and season with salt and pepper to taste.

▶ Place half of the florets stem side up in a single layer in the prepared dish. When the bottom of the pan is lined with cauliflower, spoon half the sauce over the top to coat each floret thoroughly. Add the next layer of florets stem side down. When that layer is complete, evenly spoon the remainder of the sauce over the cauliflower.

▶ Sprinkle the bread crumbs evenly over the cauliflower. Top with thinly sliced pats of butter.

▶ Bake until the top is golden brown and the sauce is bubbly, about 1 hour. Serve warm.

Serves 6 to 8.

 Cooking Tip: The sauce should pour off a spoon but be thick enough to leave a coating on the spoon. If the sauce is too thick, you can add a little milk to thin it. If the sauce is too thin, a little extra cheese will thicken it.

 Do Ahead: This casserole can be assembled the day before baking. Store covered in the refrigerator until ready to bake.

Cheddar-Pecan Green Bean Casserole

This homemade version of the classic canned-soup green bean dish is sure to become a favorite at your house. The haricots verts, pecans, and the touch of sharp cheddar in the sauce elevate this dish to new heights.

4   tablespoons unsalted butter, divided, plus extra to grease the baking dish
Kosher salt
1 1/2 pounds fresh or frozen haricots verts, trimmed
8   ounces button mushrooms, trimmed and thinly sliced
2   cloves garlic, minced
1/4 teaspoon freshly ground nutmeg

2   tablespoons all-purpose flour
3/4 cup chicken stock
3/4 cup heavy cream
1/2 cup shredded sharp white cheddar cheese
Freshly ground black pepper
3/4 cup French-fried onions
1/4 cup panko bread crumbs
1/4 cup chopped pecans

▸ Preheat the oven to 395 degrees. Lightly grease a 9- x 13-inch casserole dish with butter and set aside.

▸ Fill a large pot with water and add 1 tablespoon of salt. Over high heat, bring the salted water to a boil. Add the beans and cook until just tender, about 2 minutes. Drain and immediately plunge the beans into a large bowl of ice water to stop the cooking. Drain again and set aside.

▸ In a large saucepan over medium-high heat, melt 2 tablespoons of the butter. Add the mushrooms and cook, stirring occasionally, until the mushrooms begin to give up some of their liquid, about 5 minutes. Add the garlic and nutmeg, and cook until fragrant, about 2 minutes. Sprinkle the flour over the mushrooms and stir to combine. Slowly stir in the stock and heavy

cream. Reduce the heat to medium-low and cook, stirring frequently, until the mixture thickens, about 8 minutes. Remove from the heat and stir in the shredded cheese. Season with salt and pepper to taste. Add the green beans and stir until well coated. Spoon the mixture into the prepared pan.

▸ In a medium mixing bowl toss together the French-fried onions, bread crumbs, and pecans. In a small saucepan, melt the remaining 2 tablespoons of butter. Stir the melted butter into the onion mixture. Sprinkle the topping evenly over the green beans. Transfer to the oven and bake until golden and bubbly, about 10 to 12 minutes.

Serves 6.

 Cooking Tip: What are haricots verts? Quite simply, they are very small and slender French green beans. (*Haricot verts* is French for *green beans*.) They tend to be more tender and flavorful than the thicker, American green beans. Most markets now carry them both fresh and frozen. American green beans, fresh or frozen, are an

Creamed Spinach

The melted mozzarella topping gives this version of the classic steakhouse side dish an added richness.

1	tablespoon cornstarch
2	tablespoons milk
1	cup heavy cream
1/4	cup grated Parmesan cheese

1/4	teaspoon freshly grated nutmeg
	Kosher salt and freshly ground black pepper
2	bags (6-ounce) fresh baby spinach
1/2	cup shredded mozzarella cheese

▶ Preheat the oven to 395 degrees.

▶ In a small bowl whisk the cornstarch and milk together until smooth. Set aside.

▶ In a medium saucepan over medium-high heat, bring the cream to a boil. Remove from the heat and whisk the cornstarch mixture into the hot cream. Return the cream to the stove and cook over medium heat, whisking constantly, until the mixture thickens, about 2 minutes. Remove from the heat and stir in the Parmesan cheese and nutmeg until smooth. Season with salt and pepper to taste. Set aside.

▶ Over high heat, bring a large pot of salted water to a boil. Place the spinach in the boiling water and cook until just wilted, about 3 minutes. Drain.

▶ Add the cooked spinach to the cream sauce and stir until combined. Pour the mixture into a medium-size baking dish and sprinkle the top evenly with the mozzarella cheese. Bake until the cheese is melted and the spinach is heated through, about 15 minutes. Serve warm.

Serves 4 to 6.

 Cooking Tip: Whoever decided to make bagged salads "ready-to-eat" was a genius, in my book. Cleaning all the sand and dirt out of fresh spinach is an inconvenience I have not experienced since I found the prewashed, packaged variety. If you do choose to use the unbagged variety, be sure to clean well, remove any tough stems, and coarsely chop the leaves before adding them to the cream mixture.

Eggplant Casserole

Whenever I prepare this dish, memories of my grandmother's New Orleans kitchen come to mind. Serve it as a side dish or over a bed of rice for a satisfying main course.

2   tablespoons butter, plus extra to grease the baking dish and for the topping
1   pound small shrimp (30/40 count), peeled and deveined
2   teaspoons Cajun seasoning
Kosher salt
4   large eggplants
4   slices bacon, cut into 1/2-inch slices
1   cup finely diced yellow onion (1 large onion)
1   cup finely diced green bell pepper (1 large pepper)

1/2   cup thinly sliced celery (about 2 ribs)
2   tablespoons tomato paste
1/4   teaspoon cayenne pepper
1   tablespoon dried oregano
1   tablespoon dried thyme
3   bay leaves
Freshly ground black pepper
1   cup plain bread crumbs

▶ Preheat the oven to 350 degrees. Lightly grease a 21/2-quart baking dish with butter and set aside.

▶ Place the shrimp in a large mixing bowl and toss with the Cajun seasoning. Refrigerate while cooking the eggplants.

▶ Fill a large stockpot with water and add 1 tablespoon of salt. Over high heat, bring the salted water to a boil. Add the whole eggplants and cook until fork tender, about 15 to 20 minutes. Drain and place on a rimmed baking sheet. Slice the eggplants open lengthwise and let rest until cool enough to handle.

▶ In a large skillet over medium-high heat, cook the bacon until crispy, about 4 minutes. With a slotted spoon, transfer the bacon to a paper towel–lined plate to drain.

▶ Pour all but 2 tablespoons of fat from the skillet. Reduce the heat to medium. Add the onion, bell pepper, and celery. Cook, stirring until soft, about 6 minutes. Add the tomato paste, stirring to evenly coat the vegetables, and cook until the flavors have melded, about 2 minutes.

▶ Using a spoon, scoop the flesh from the eggplant skins and add to the pan. Discard the skins and pour any excess juices left on the baking sheet into the pan. Add the cayenne, oregano, thyme, and bay leaves. Cook, stirring with a wooden spoon to break up the eggplant, until the flavors have melded, about 20 minutes. Season with salt and pepper to taste. Add the cooked bacon.

▶ In a separate pan over medium heat, melt 2 tablespoons of butter. Add the shrimp and sauté, turning occasionally, until cooked through, about 4 minutes. Transfer the shrimp to the eggplant mixture and stir to combine.

▸ Pour the eggplant mixture into the prepared baking dish. Sprinkle the bread crumbs evenly over the eggplant. Top with thinly sliced pats of butter.

▸ Bake until the top is golden brown and the sauce is bubbly, about 1 hour. Serve warm.

Serves 8.

 Cooking Tip: If your bread crumbs are browning too quickly, cover the dish lightly with foil.

 Variation: Omit the shrimp and bacon for a vegetarian version.

Glazed Carrots

This classic French technique is how I learned to prepare root vegetables while I was in cooking school. The technique is so simple yet makes an ordinary carrot something special.

3   cups peeled and thinly sliced carrots (about 5 carrots)

2   tablespoons unsalted butter

1   tablespoon granulated sugar
Kosher salt and freshly ground black pepper

▶ Place the carrots, butter, and sugar in a medium pot. Pour in enough water to barely cover the vegetables. Season with salt and pepper to taste.

▶ Over high heat, bring the mixture to a boil. Reduce the heat to medium-low and cook, simmering, until most of the liquid has evaporated and the carrots are tender, about 8 minutes. If the carrots are not fully cooked, add a little more water and continue cooking until they are tender. Remove from the heat and adjust the seasonings as needed. Serve immediately.

Serves 4.

 Cooking Tip: This cooking technique is great for root vegetables, like carrots, parsnips, turnips, and onions. If you plan to serve a medley of vegetables, it is better to glaze each type separately and then toss together just before serving.

Herb-Roasted Winter Vegetables

Winter vegetables never taste, or look, as good as when they are roasted together with fresh herbs. I like to use beets, acorn squash, turnips, parsnips, and rutabagas for the ultimate mixture of colors and flavors.

1/2	cup olive oil, divided, plus extra to grease the baking sheet
3	red beets, peeled and cut into small wedges
2	tablespoons chopped fresh thyme, divided
	Kosher salt and freshly ground black pepper
4	shallots, peeled and quartered
1	acorn squash, unpeeled, halved, seeded and cut into 1/2-inch wedges
1	turnip, peeled and cut into wedges
2	parsnips, peeled and cut into small pieces
1	rutabaga, peeled and cut into wedges
6	cloves garlic, peeled

▶ Preheat oven to 425 degrees. Lightly grease a rimmed baking sheet with olive oil and set aside.

▶ In a small bowl toss together the beets, a large pinch of thyme, and 1 tablespoon of the olive oil. Season with salt and pepper to taste. Place on one corner of the prepared pan.

▶ In a large mixing bowl toss together the shallots, squash, turnips, parsnips, rutabaga, garlic, the remaining thyme, and the remaining olive oil. Season with salt and pepper to taste. Spread the vegetables in a single layer on the prepared pan, away from the beets.

▶ Roast the vegetables, stirring occasionally, being sure to keep the beets separate, until all the vegetables are tender, about 45 to 60 minutes. Stir in the beets. Adjust the seasonings as needed. Serve warm.

Serves 6 to 8.

 Cooking Tip: Fresh beets will turn everything red if they are roasted with the other vegetables. That is why I recommend roasting them in a separate part of the pan. For minimal mess, wrap whole unpeeled beets in aluminum foil and roast until easily pierced with the tip of a knife. Using paper towels, remove the peel from the beets. Cut into small wedges and toss with the other roasted vegetables.

 Variation: You can use any combination of winter vegetables that you prefer, including carrots, butternut squash, cipollini onions, and potatoes.

Lemony Swiss Chard with Pine Nuts and Raisins

With its bright green leaves and stems of yellow, orange, and red, rainbow Swiss chard is by far the prettiest green around. Be sure not to overcook because its flavor is best when it is just lightly sautéed.

2	tablespoons olive oil		1	tablespoon finely grated lemon zest
2	tablespoons finely diced shallots		1/4	cup golden raisins
6	cups coarsely chopped rainbow Swiss chard leaves		1/4	cup pine nuts, toasted
1	tablespoon freshly squeezed lemon juice			Kosher salt and freshly ground black pepper
1	tablespoon water			

▶ In a large skillet over medium-high heat, warm the oil until a few droplets of water sizzle when carefully sprinkled in the skillet. Add the shallots and cook until they are soft, about 2 minutes.

▶ Add the chard and cook, stirring, until the leaves just begin to wilt, about 1 minute. Stir in the lemon juice, water, lemon zest, and raisins. Cover and cook, stirring occasionally, until the chard is tender and the liquid has almost evaporated, about 5 minutes. Remove from the heat and stir in the pine nuts. Season with salt and pepper to taste. Serve immediately.

Serves 4.

 Cooking Tip: I prefer rainbow Swiss chard due to its brightly colored veins, but varieties with only white or red veins are equally delicious.

 Variation: For more texture and color, use the stems in this dish as well. Cut the stems into 1/2-inch pieces, add to the pan before adding the leaves, and cook until the stems are tender, about 2 to 3 minutes. Then add the leaves and continue with the recipe.

Parmesan Roasted Tomatoes

Roasting tomatoes gives them that rich summer flavor year-round.

1/2 cup panko bread crumbs
2 tablespoons freshly grated Parmesan cheese
1 clove garlic, minced
2 tablespoons finely chopped fresh
flat-leaf parsley

1/2 teaspoon dried oregano
6 large ripe tomatoes, cut in half horizontally
Kosher salt and freshly ground black pepper
2 tablespoons olive oil

▶ Preheat the oven to 395 degrees.

▶ In a medium mixing bowl stir together the bread crumbs, Parmesan cheese, garlic, parsley, and oregano until well combined. Place the tomato halves in a shallow baking dish, sliced side up. Season the tomatoes with salt and pepper to taste. Sprinkle the tops of the tomatoes with the Parmesan bread crumb mixture. Drizzle the olive oil evenly over the tomatoes.

▶ Bake until the topping is golden, about 20 minutes. Serve warm.

Serves 6.

 Variation: You can use Roma or cherry tomatoes for this recipe as well.

Ratatouille

Ratatouille is a classic French dish composed of eggplant, peppers, zucchini, and basil. Toss this delicious vegetable stew with cooked ziti or penne pasta for a vegetarian entree.

1 medium eggplant, cubed (about 3 cups)	1 cup diced yellow squash (about 2 small squash)
Kosher salt	1½ cups diced tomatoes (about 4 tomatoes)
3 tablespoons olive oil	Freshly ground black pepper
½ cup thinly sliced yellow onion (1 small onion)	⅓ cup chopped fresh basil
½ cup diced red bell pepper (1 small pepper)	
2 cloves garlic, minced	
1½ cups diced zucchini (about 3 small zucchinis)	

▸ Place the eggplant in a colander and sprinkle with salt. Let the eggplant drain in the colander for 1 hour, rinse, and then pat dry.

▸ In a large sauce pot or Dutch oven over medium-high heat, warm the oil until a few droplets of water sizzle when carefully sprinkled in the pot. Add the eggplant and cook, stirring often, until golden, about 3 to 4 minutes. Add the onion and pepper and cook until soft, about 4 minutes. Add the garlic, zucchini, squash, and tomatoes. Cook until a soft stew has formed, about 20 minutes. Season with salt and pepper to taste. Remove from the heat and fold in the basil. Serve immediately.

Serves 4 to 6.

 Cooking Tips: Sometimes it can be difficult to find good tomatoes in the winter. A drained 14.5-ounce can of diced tomatoes is a perfect substitute.

Salting eggplant removes bitterness. If cooking fresh in-season eggplant (summer months), you can omit this step.

Sautéed Shiitake Mushrooms

Sautéed mushrooms make an excellent side dish or garnish for cooked meats. I use shiitakes in this version, but feel free to use any combination of exotic and common mushrooms that you find in your market.

1 tablespoon olive oil	1 clove garlic, minced
2 tablespoons finely diced shallots	1 teaspoon dried thyme
1 tablespoon unsalted butter	Kosher salt and freshly ground black pepper
1 pound shiitake mushrooms, cleaned, stems removed and discarded, and thinly sliced	

▸ In a large skillet over medium-high heat, warm the oil until a few droplets of water sizzle when carefully sprinkled in the skillet. Add the shallots and cook until they are soft, about 1 minute. Add the butter and allow it to melt. Once the butter starts to foam, add the mushrooms, garlic, and thyme. Cook, stirring often, until lightly browned, about 5 to 7 minutes. Season with salt and pepper to taste. Serve warm.

Serves 4.

 Cooking Tip: Never soak mushrooms in water; they will absorb the liquid like a sponge. To clean, lightly brush off any dirt with a damp paper towel or with a small brush.

Sautéed Spaghetti Squash

Spaghetti squash is the craziest vegetable! When you cook it, the flesh looks like strands of spaghetti. In fact, some people even use it in lieu of spaghetti noodles. This dish lets the sweet flavor of this gourd take center stage.

1 medium spaghetti squash (about 3 pounds)	2 tablespoons unsalted butter
2 tablespoons olive oil	2 cloves garlic, minced
Kosher salt and freshly ground black pepper	1 teaspoon crushed red pepper flakes

▸ Preheat the oven to 375 degrees.

▸ Cut the spaghetti squash in half lengthwise and scoop out the seeds. Brush each half with olive oil and season with salt and pepper. Place the halves flesh side down on a rimmed baking sheet and bake until the outside of the squash can be easily pierced by a fork, about 1 hour. Remove from the oven.

▸ Using a fork, scrape the flesh out of the squash, loosening and separating the strands as you remove it from the skin. Set the flesh aside and discard the skins.

▸ Melt the butter in a large skillet over medium heat. Add the garlic and cook, stirring, until fragrant, about 1 minute. Add the squash and stir to combine. Sprinkle in the red pepper flakes. Season with salt and pepper to taste. Cook until the squash is warmed through, about 3 to 5 minutes. Serve warm.

Serves 4 to 6.

 Do Ahead: The squash can be roasted in advance and sautéed just before serving.

 Time-Saving Tip: Roasting the squash in the oven gives it a rich, caramelized flavor, but if you are short on time, the squash can be cooked in the microwave. Cut the spaghetti squash in half lengthwise and scoop out the seeds. Place on a microwave-safe plate, flesh side down. Cook on high until the outside of the squash can be easily pierced by a fork, about 15 minutes.

Succotash

Sufferin' succotash! You will be surprised at how yummy this simple veggie dish is. If available, use fresh corn or lima beans, but I just love the convenience of the frozen veggies for last-minute suppers.

2	tablespoons unsalted butter
2	cups frozen corn kernels, thawed
1 1/2	cups frozen lima beans, thawed
1/4	cup thinly sliced scallions
1/2	cup heavy cream
1/4	cup water
	Kosher salt and freshly ground black pepper

▸ In a large saucepan over medium heat, melt the butter. Add the corn, lima beans, and scallions. Cook, stirring often, until warmed through, about 2 minutes. Add the heavy cream and water. Over high heat, bring the mixture to a boil and reduce the heat to medium-low. Cook, simmering, until the sauce has thickened, about 10 minutes. Season with salt and pepper to taste. Serve warm.

Serves 4 to 6.

 Cooking Tip: Need a lighter version? Substitute chicken or vegetable stock for the cream. You can also substitute protein-packed shelled edamame for the limas.

Yellow Squash Casserole

Last summer, Memphis Farmers Market founding board member Linda Cornish gave me her yellow squash recipe when I was lamenting over not knowing what to do with the bounty of yellow squash from my garden. This is my version of her delicious concoction.

5   tablespoons unsalted butter, plus extra to grease the baking dish and for the topping

2   pounds yellow summer squash (about 8 squash)

Kosher salt

3/4   cup finely diced yellow onion (1 medium onion)

1   clove garlic, minced

1   small jalapeño pepper, seeded and finely diced

1¹/2   cups panko bread crumbs, divided

4   large eggs, lightly beaten

1   container (15-ounce) whole-milk or part-skim ricotta cheese

1   small log (4-ounce) fresh goat cheese

1/2   cup grated Parmesan cheese, divided

1/4   teaspoon paprika

Freshly ground black pepper

▸ Preheat the oven to 375 degrees. Lightly grease a 2¹/2-quart baking dish with butter and set aside.

▸ Cut the squash into ¹/2-inch thick slices. Over high heat, bring a large pot of salted water to a boil. Add the squash and cook until fork tender, about 10 minutes. Drain well. Transfer to the bowl of a food processor and coarsely puree.

▸ In a large saucepot over medium heat, melt the butter. Add the onion, garlic, and jalapeño pepper. Cook until soft but not browned, about 4 minutes.

Add the squash puree, 1 cup of the bread crumbs, the eggs, the ricotta cheese, goat cheese, ¹/4 cup of the Parmesan cheese, and the paprika. Season with salt and pepper to taste. Stir until well combined. Pour the puree into the prepared baking dish and top with the remaining ¹/2 cup of bread crumbs, ¹/4 cup of Parmesan, and thinly sliced pats of butter. Bake until golden brown, about 40 minutes.

Serves 6 to 8.

 Cooking Tip: Panko bread crumbs, also known as Japanese bread crumbs, have a crispier, lighter texture than traditional American bread crumbs.

SWEET ENDINGS

Opposite page: Coconut Cake (page 210)

Banana Pudding Pie

If you saw me on the Food Network's show Dinner Impossible, *you know that chef Robert Irvine and I disagreed on how to make Southern banana pudding. Robert, this one is for you!*

For the Crust:

2   cups vanilla wafer cookies, plus extra for the pie garnish

1/4   cup granulated sugar

4   tablespoons (1/2 stick) unsalted butter, melted and cooled to room temperature

For the Filling:

2   cups heavy cream

1/3   cup cornstarch

1/4   teaspoon salt

3   large egg yolks

1/2   cup granulated sugar

1   teaspoon pure vanilla extract

3   ripe bananas

For the Whipped Cream Topping:

1   cup heavy cream, chilled

1/4   cup granulated or powdered sugar

1   teaspoon pure vanilla extract

▸ Preheat the oven to 325 degrees.

▸ To make the crust: In a food processor, finely grind the cookies. Add the sugar and pulse until combined. Slowly add the butter and pulse until well incorporated and moist clumps form. Transfer to a 9-inch tart pan with a removable bottom. Press the crust evenly into the bottom and up the sides. Bake until set, about 8 minutes. Cool completely on a wire rack.

▸ To make the filling: In a medium saucepan, combine the cream, cornstarch, salt, egg yolks, sugar, and vanilla. Over medium-low heat, cook, whisking continuously, until the mixture thickens, about 10 minutes. Remove from the heat and transfer to a large mixing bowl. Place in the refrigerator and cool completely, about 1 hour.

▸ Spoon half of the cooled pudding evenly over the bottom of the crust. Peel the bananas and cut into 1/4-inch thick slices. Create a layer of banana slices, reserving some for garnish. Spoon the remaining pudding evenly over the bananas. Place the pie in the refrigerator to set while making the whipped cream topping.

▸ To make the topping: In the bowl of an electric mixer, whip the cream, sugar, and vanilla until soft peaks form. Spoon or use a pastry bag to pipe the whipped cream evenly over the pie filling. Chill the pie until set, at least 4 hours. Before serving, garnish with the remaining banana slices and extra vanilla wafer cookies.

Serves 8.

 Do Ahead: You can make and refrigerate this crust and the pie filling the day before. Add the whipped cream and garnishes up to 6 hours before you serve it.

 Time-Saving Tip: Instant vanilla pudding can be substituted in a pinch, but the homemade version only takes a few more minutes and tastes much better.

Blueberry Almond Crumble

Crumble versus cobbler? The difference is in the topping. Crumbles have a crumbly streusel-like topping, while cobblers have a pastry or biscuit topping. Both are irresistible ways to use fresh fruit.

For the Filling:

6   cups blueberries, fresh or frozen
     (frozen berries need to be thawed)
1/2 cup granulated sugar
2   tablespoons cornstarch
1   teaspoon finely grated lemon zest
1   tablespoon freshly squeezed lemon juice

For the Topping:

1   cup all-purpose flour
1/2 cup old-fashioned rolled oats (not instant)
1/2 cup slivered almonds
1/2 teaspoon baking powder
1/2 teaspoon Kosher salt
6   tablespoons (3/4 stick) unsalted butter,
     room temperature
1/2 cup granulated sugar
Vanilla ice cream (optional)

▶ Preheat the oven to 375 degrees.

▶ To make the filling: In a large mixing bowl place the blueberries, sugar, cornstarch, lemon zest, and lemon juice. Gently toss to combine. Transfer the filling to a 2-quart baking dish and set aside while you make the topping.

▶ To make the topping: In a medium mixing bowl stir together the flour, oats, almonds, baking powder, and salt. In the bowl of an electric mixer fitted with the paddle attachment, beat the butter and sugar until

light and fluffy. Add the dry ingredients and mix until just combined and small clumps form. (Be careful not to overmix.). Crumble the topping evenly over the filling. In case of overflow, place the baking dish on a rimmed baking sheet. Bake the crumble until the fruit juices bubble up around the edges of the baking dish and the topping turns golden brown, about 45 minutes. Let cool slightly before serving warm, with a scoop of vanilla ice cream, if desired.

Serves 8.

 Cooking Tip: Crumbles work well with all types of fruit. Consider using this topping on fillings made from fresh berries, apples, pears, or cherries.

 Back-to-the-Basics: For a nut-free topping, substitute an additional 1/4 cup of oats.

 Time-Saving Tip: This crumble topping freezes well. My sister always has frozen fruit and prepared crumble topping in her freezer to serve dessert for impromptu guests. Store the topping in an airtight container for up to 3 months.

Buttermilk Pie

This pie should be called "easy as pie" buttermilk pie. My friend Kelly Thompson's grandmother, Delma Huckeba, came up with this recipe back in the 1960s because she had had no luck making pies with meringue. It was an instant hit and has been served at every one of her family gatherings since then! It is truly a delicious "no-fail" pie.

1   unbaked pie crust (9-inch), homemade or store-bought
1½ cups granulated sugar
3   tablespoons all-purpose flour
1   cup buttermilk

1   tablespoon freshly squeezed lemon juice
2   teaspoons pure vanilla extract
2   large eggs
½   cup (1 stick) unsalted butter, melted and cooled to room temperature

▸ Preheat the oven to 415 degrees.

▸ Place the pie crust in a deep-dish pie pan and flute the edges, if desired. Set aside.

▸ In a large mixing bowl whisk together the sugar, flour, buttermilk, lemon juice, vanilla, eggs, and melted butter.

▸ Bake the pie crust until light golden brown, about 5 minutes. Remove the pie crust from the oven and pour the filling into the warm crust. Return the pie to the oven and bake until warmed, about 10 minutes. Then, without opening the door, reduce the heat to 350 degrees and bake until set, about 40 minutes.

▸ Remove from the oven, place on a wire rack, and cool completely. Serve at room temperature.

Serves 8.

 Cooking Tip: Be sure not to remove the pie from the oven too early, or you will have pudding, not pie, for dessert! A perfectly baked buttermilk pie should be firm with a golden top and a lightly browned crust.

 Freezes Well.

Chocolate Brownie Sundaes

Warm, chocolaty brownies topped with creamy vanilla ice cream and an ooey-gooey hot fudge sauce . . . need I say more?

10	tablespoons unsalted butter, plus extra to grease the pan
1/2	cup all-purpose flour, plus extra to flour the pan
1/4	cup unsweetened cocoa powder
1/4	teaspoon salt
1/4	teaspoon baking powder
8	ounces bittersweet chocolate, coarsely chopped

1 1/2	cups granulated sugar
4	large eggs
1	teaspoon pure vanilla extract
3/4	cup semisweet chocolate chips
1	pint vanilla ice cream
2	cups hot fudge sauce

▸ Preheat the oven to 350 degrees. Butter and lightly flour an 8- x 8-inch metal baking pan. Sift the flour, cocoa powder, salt, and baking powder into a small bowl. Set aside.

▸ In a double boiler over medium heat, melt the butter and chopped chocolate, stirring until smooth. Remove from the heat and let cool slightly, about 5 minutes.

▸ In a large mixing bowl whisk the sugar, eggs, and vanilla until well blended. Stir in the melted chocolate mixture. Add the flour mixture and stir until just blended. Fold in the chocolate chips.

▸ Pour the batter into the prepared pan. Bake until a toothpick inserted into the center comes out clean, about 50 to 55 minutes. Cool for 10 minutes and cut into squares.

▸ Top the brownies with a scoop of vanilla ice cream and hot fudge sauce.

Serves 6.

 Cooking Tips: Homemade hot fudge sauce is so easy to make. Place 10 ounces of chopped bittersweet chocolate in a heatproof bowl. In a small saucepot over medium-high heat, bring 1 1/2 cups of heavy cream to a boil. Pour the scalded cream over the chocolate and let it sit for 1 minute to melt the chocolate. Whisk the mixture together until smooth. The sauce can be stored in the refrigerator for up to 1 week. Reheat in a double boiler or microwave.

Lining the bottom of the baking pan with parchment paper makes it easy to remove the brownies.

 Variation: This recipe makes very thick brownies. For a thinner brownie, bake the batter in a 9- x 13-inch metal baking pan for 30 to 35 minutes.

Coconut Cake

This truly is the best coconut cake ever! The recipe, which originated in the kitchen of June Rodgers, was shared with me by her daughter, Linda Wray, and granddaughter, Lee Anne. Be forewarned: you can't have just one piece of this decadently moist coconut cake.

For the Cake:

1/2 cup vegetable oil, plus extra to grease the pan

All-purpose flour, to flour the pan

2 packages (6-ounce) frozen fresh coconut

1 container (8-ounce) sour cream

1 1/2 cups granulated sugar

1 box (18-ounce) yellow cake mix

1 box (4-ounce) instant vanilla pudding mix

1 cup water

1 teaspoon pure vanilla extract

2 large eggs

2 large egg yolks

1 can (15-ounce) cream of coconut

For the Icing:

1 cup granulated sugar

1/2 cup water

2 egg whites

3 cups sweetened shredded coconut

▶ To make the cake: Preheat the oven to 350 degrees. Grease and flour two 9-inch cake pans and set aside.

▶ In a medium mixing bowl whisk together the frozen coconut, sour cream, and sugar. Set aside.

▶ In a the bowl of an electric mixer, combine the yellow cake mix, vanilla pudding mix, 1/2 cup oil, water, vanilla extract, eggs, egg yolks, and cream of coconut. Beat the mixture until smooth. Pour the batter, dividing it equally, into the prepared cake pans. Bake until the cakes are golden brown and a toothpick inserted into the center comes out clean, about 30 minutes.

▶ Remove the cakes from the oven and cool in the pans on wire racks just until cool enough to handle, about 10 minutes. Remove the cakes from the pans and place onto wire racks.

▶ Carefully slice each of the warm cakes in half horizontally to make a total of 4 thin layers. Place one of the 4 layers on a serving plate. Spread one-third of the sour cream–coconut mixture evenly on top. Continue with layering the remaining cake layers and sour cream–coconut mixture. Transfer the cake to the refrigerator to cool at least 20 minutes.

▶ To make the icing: In a small saucepot whisk together the sugar and water until the sugar has dissolved. Over high heat, bring the mixture to a boil and cook without stirring until it reaches a temperature of 235 degrees, or when it forms long threads when poured from a spoon back into the pot, about 10 minutes. Remove the sugar syrup from the heat and set aside. Do not cool the sugar syrup.

▶ In the bowl of an electric mixer, beat the egg whites on high speed until they hold soft peaks. While continuing to beat, slowly pour the hot sugar syrup into the egg whites. Continue to beat on high until the icing is shiny and has cooled, about 4 to 5 minutes.

▸ Frost the top and sides of the cake. Generously sprinkle the shredded coconut all over the cake. Refrigerate overnight before serving.

Serves 8 to 10.

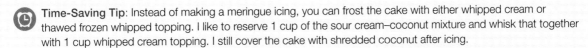

Time-Saving Tip: Instead of making a meringue icing, you can frost the cake with either whipped cream or thawed frozen whipped topping. I like to reserve 1 cup of the sour cream–coconut mixture and whisk that together with 1 cup whipped cream topping. I still cover the cake with shredded coconut after icing.

Cooking Tips: This recipe uses coconut in three forms. Found on the baking aisle, sweetened shredded coconut is the most common. It is flaked coconut that has been soaked in corn syrup for added sweetness and moisture. Frozen fresh coconut is just what it's called: fresh coconut that has been flaked and frozen. It is found next to the frozen fruit in most markets. If you cannot find it, you can substitute sweetened shredded coconut. Cream of coconut is a thick sweet liquid made from coconuts. Often used to make drinks, it is found in the mixer section of your grocery or liquor store. Coconut milk is not a substitute.

When making the cake batter, save the egg whites for the icing.

See picture on page 200.

Crème Brulee

There is nothing more delicious than a creamy custard topped with a crunchy layer of caramelized sugar. With just five ingredients, you will be shocked at how easy this popular "restaurant" dessert is to make at home.

4	cups (1 quart) heavy cream
¾	cup granulated sugar, plus extra for the tops of the custards

8	large egg yolks
1	teaspoon pure vanilla extract
2	tablespoons orange liqueur

▶ Preheat the oven to 325 degrees.

▶ In a large saucepot over medium-high heat, warm the heavy cream until just below the boiling point. Remove from the heat and set aside.

▶ In a large heatproof bowl, stir the sugar, egg yolks, vanilla, and liqueur together until just blended. Gradually stir in the hot cream until the sugar has dissolved. Strain the custard through a fine sieve into eight 6- to 8-ounce ovenproof ramekins.

▶ Arrange the ramekins in a roasting pan with at least 2-inch sides. Place the pan on the middle rack of the oven. Very carefully pour enough hot water around the ramekins to come halfway up the sides of the ramekins. Slide the rack into the oven, being careful not to slosh water onto the custards. Bake until the custards are set, about 1 hour. Remove the custards from the water bath, cool to room temperature, and chill in the refrigerator until set, at least 2 hours.

▶ Just before serving, sprinkle about 1 tablespoon of granulated sugar evenly across the tops of each of the chilled custards. Heat the sugar with a kitchen blowtorch until the sugar caramelizes evenly. (If you do not have a kitchen blowtorch, add a splash of liqueur to the sugar and flambé with a match.)

Serves 8.

 Cooking Tips: The custards are set when they are firm when gently shaken. If you are uncertain, you can test the custard by poking the tip of a knife into it. The custard is ready when the knife comes out clean.

It is often a feat to create a water bath without making a mess. Try using a teakettle to heat and pour the hot water for a more controlled pour.

 Do Ahead: The custards can be baked the day before. Wait until the last minute to caramelize the sugar on top, or the crust will lose its crunch.

 Back-to-the-Basics: For a classic vanilla crème brulee, you can omit the orange liqueur and add 1 additional teaspoon of vanilla instead.

Double-Decker Peach Cobbler

When Laurie Major told me about her grandmother's peach cobbler, I just had to give it a try. Mrs. Mohler made it with three layers of crust! I am all about the crust but am a little lazy at times. I have made this into a double-decker cobbler. But if you have an extra 10 or 15 minutes, you can add that third layer of pastry.

4	tablespoons (1/2 stick) unsalted butter, plus extra to grease the baking dish
1	cup granulated sugar, divided
1/2	cup water
2	bags (16-ounce) frozen peaches, thawed, or 12 ripe peaches, peeled, pitted, and sliced (about 5 to 6 cups)
2	teaspoons freshly squeezed lemon juice
2	tablespoons bourbon

3	teaspoons ground cinnamon, divided
1/4	teaspoon freshly grated nutmeg
	Pinch of salt
1/4	cup all-purpose flour
2	unbaked pie crusts (9-inch), homemade or store-bought
1	large egg, lightly beaten
1	pint vanilla ice cream (optional)

▶ Preheat the oven to 400 degrees. Lightly grease a 2-quart baking dish with butter and set aside.

▶ In a large saucepot over medium heat, melt the butter. Add 3/4 cup of the sugar and water. Cook, stirring, until the sugar is dissolved. Add the peaches, lemon juice, bourbon, 2 teaspoons of the cinnamon, nutmeg, and salt. Cook, stirring occasionally, until the flavors have melded, about 5 minutes. Add the flour, stir to coat, and cook until the sauce is slightly thickened, about 2 to 3 minutes.

▶ Evenly spoon half of the filling into the prepared dish. Top with a layer of pie crust. Bake until lightly browned, about 15 minutes. Remove from the oven, and spoon the remaining filling evenly over the crust. Top with the second pie crust. Brush the top crust with the beaten egg. Evenly sprinkle the remaining 1/4 cup of sugar and the remaining 1 teaspoon of cinnamon over the top. Bake until the crust is golden brown and the filling is bubbly, about 18 to 20 minutes.

▶ Serve warm, with a scoop of vanilla ice cream if desired.

Serves 8.

 Variation: To make the third layer, place a pie crust on the bottom of the pan. Par-bake the bottom crust for 10 minutes. Then layer as directed in the recipe above.

 Time-Saving Tip: I love fresh peaches, but they can be a hassle to peel. Frozen peaches are in season year-round and work just as well in this dish . . . without the extra work!

 Freezes Well.

Glazed Lemon Pound Cake

My good friend Kristen Keegan won "Best in Show" at the Mid-South Fair with this cake. Moist and delicious, it has just the perfect amount of lemony flavor. Serve it on its own or with freshly whipped cream and fresh berries.

For the Cake:

- 1/2 cup (1 stick) salted butter, softened, plus extra to grease the loaf pan
- 1 1/2 cups all-purpose flour, plus extra to flour the loaf pan
- 1/4 teaspoon baking powder
- 1/4 teaspoon salt
- 1/4 cup butter-flavor all-vegetable shortening
- 1 1/2 cups granulated sugar
- 3 large eggs
- 1/2 cup milk
- 1/2 teaspoon pure vanilla extract
- 1/2 teaspoon lemon extract
- 1 tablespoon freshly grated lemon zest

For the Lemon Glaze:

- 3 tablespoons unsalted butter, melted
- 1/2 cup granulated sugar
- 3 tablespoons freshly squeezed lemon juice
- 2 tablespoons water

▸ To make the cake: Preheat the oven to 325 degrees. Grease and flour a 9 x 5-inch loaf pan.

▸ In a medium mixing bowl, combine the flour, baking powder, and salt. Set aside.

▸ In the bowl of an electric mixer, beat the butter, shortening, and sugar until light and fluffy. Add the eggs and mix until well combined. Add the reserved flour mixture and mix until well blended. Add the milk, vanilla extract, lemon extract, and lemon zest. Stir to blend. Spoon the batter into the prepared pan. Bake until a toothpick inserted into the center comes out clean, about 60 to 70 minutes. While it is still in the pan, pierce several holes in the cake with a knife or skewer. Prepare the glaze and top before the cake is completely cooled or removed from the pan.

▸ To make the glaze: In a small bowl combine the melted butter, sugar, lemon juice, and water. Stir until the sugar has dissolved, about 1 to 2 minutes. Pour the glaze over the cake and let the cake sit in the pan until the glaze is fully absorbed, about 20 minutes.

▸ Remove from the pan and transfer to a serving plate. Serve at room temperature.

Serves 8.

 Cooking Tips: Cooking for a crowd? You can easily double this recipe and bake it in a Bundt pan.

For 1 tablespoon of freshly grated lemon zest, you will need 1 large (or 2 small) lemons. For no waste, first zest your lemons and then juice them.

 Freezes Well.

Hot Cocoa Chocolate Pudding

This pudding isn't really served hot, but the richness from using both cocoa powder and bittersweet chocolate remind me of the indulgent flavor of a good cup of hot chocolate.

2	cups heavy cream
1/4	cup cornstarch
1/4	teaspoon salt
6	large egg yolks
1/2	cup granulated sugar
3	tablespoons unsweetened cocoa powder

1	ounce bittersweet chocolate, coarsely chopped
1	tablespoon unsalted butter
1	tablespoon pure vanilla extract
Whipped cream (optional)	

▶ In a medium saucepan, combine the cream, cornstarch, salt, egg yolks, sugar, and cocoa powder. Over medium-low heat, cook, whisking continuously, until the mixture thickens, about 10 minutes.

▶ Remove from the heat and stir in the chopped chocolate, butter, and vanilla extract. Stir until the chocolate and butter are melted and well combined. Transfer to six 6-ounce ramekins. Cool to room temperature and transfer to the refrigerator until chilled, about 1 hour. Serve with a dollop of whipped cream, if desired.

Serves 4 to 6.

 Do Ahead: The pudding can be made a day ahead, covered, and refrigerated.

 Variation: For a less-decadent version, you can substitute whole milk for the heavy cream.

 Cooking Tip: The texture of this rich, decadent pudding is similar to that of a thick custard.

Peanut Butter Cup Tart

Peanut butter and chocolate is a marriage made in heaven, in my opinion. This tart is my twist on the delicious peanut butter cup candy.

For the Crust:

- 1 box (9-ounce) chocolate wafer cookies, crumbled
- 2 ounces bittersweet chocolate, coarsely chopped
- 5 tablespoons unsalted butter, melted and cooled to room temperature

For the Filling:

- 8 ounces cream cheese, room temperature
- 1 cup creamy peanut butter
- 1/2 cup granulated sugar
- 1 teaspoon pure vanilla extract
- 1 cup heavy cream

For the Topping:

- 4 ounces semisweet chocolate, finely chopped
- 1 tablespoon unsalted butter
- 1/2 cup heavy cream
- 6 peanut butter cups, coarsely chopped

▸ Preheat the oven to 325 degrees.

▸ To make the crust: In a food processor, finely grind the cookies and the chocolate. Add the butter and pulse until well incorporated and moist clumps form. Transfer to a 9-inch tart pan with a removable bottom. Press the crust evenly into the bottom and up the side. Bake until set, about 8 minutes. Cool completely on a wire rack.

▸ To make the filling: In the bowl of an electric mixer, beat the cream cheese, peanut butter, sugar, and vanilla until light and fluffy. In another bowl, whip 1 cup of the heavy cream until stiff. Fold the whipped cream into the cream cheese mixture until well combined. Evenly spoon the filling into the cooled crust. Place the tart in the refrigerator to set while making the topping.

▸ To make the topping: Place the chocolate and butter in a medium heatproof bowl. In a small saucepan over medium-high heat, bring the 1/2 cup of cream just to a boil. Immediately pour the hot cream over the chocolate and butter. Let stand for 30 seconds, then whisk until smooth and all the chocolate has melted.

▸ Carefully pour the chocolate topping evenly over the pie. Garnish the edges with the chopped peanut butter cups. Refrigerate, uncovered, until set, at least 4 hours.

Serves 8 to 10.

Cooking Tips: Chocolate wafer cookies are basically the chocolate cookie part of an Oreo®. The most popular brand is the Nabisco® Famous™ Chocolate Cookie Wafers. You should be able to find them in the cookie, baking, or ice cream department at your local market. If for some reason you can't find them, you can use Oreo® cookies with the cream filling scraped off. You will need about 3 cups of cookie crumbs.

Folding is a technique to blend a whipped ingredient (such as whipped cream or whipped egg whites) into a mixture to prevent the whipped ingredient from deflating. To fold, you take part of the mixture and bring it up and over, basically "folding" the ingredients over each other until well incorporated.

Praline Bread Pudding

Heather Bugg Ries was one of the first employees at my old restaurant, Cheffie's Market & More. After a stint in our bakery, Heather went on to culinary school. I am proud to say she is now an accomplished pastry chef. This is my simplified rendition of her to-die-for bread pudding.

For the Bread Pudding:

Unsalted butter, to grease the baking dish
1   cup milk
1   cup heavy cream
1/2 cup firmly packed dark brown sugar
2   large eggs
2   large egg yolks
1   teaspoon pure vanilla extract
1/2 teaspoon ground cinnamon
1/2 teaspoon freshly grated nutmeg
6   large croissants, 1 day old, cut in 1-inch cubes and set aside in a large mixing bowl (about 8 cups)
2   cups coarsely chopped praline pecans

For the Praline Sauce:

1   cup dark brown sugar
1/4 teaspoon baking soda
1/4 teaspoon pure vanilla extract
1   tablespoon dark corn syrup
1/2 cup buttermilk
1/2 cup (1 stick) unsalted butter, cubed
Pinch of salt

▶ To make the bread pudding: Preheat the oven to 375 degrees. Lightly grease a 9- x 13-inch baking dish with butter and set aside.

▶ In a large mixing bowl combine the milk, cream, brown sugar, eggs, egg yolks, vanilla, cinnamon, and nutmeg. Whisk until combined. Pour the pudding over the croissants, and coat evenly. Let stand until the croissants have soaked up the pudding, about 5 minutes. Stir in the praline pecan pieces.

▶ Pour the mixture into the prepared baking dish and cover with aluminum foil.

▶ Place the dish in a roasting pan with at least 2-inch sides. Place the pan on the middle rack of the oven.

Very carefully pour enough hot water around the dish to come halfway up the sides of the baking dish. Slide the rack into the oven, being careful not to slosh water onto the bread pudding. Bake until set, about 25 minutes. Remove the foil and bake until the bread pudding is puffed and golden brown on top, about 15 to 20 minutes.

▶ To make the praline sauce: In a medium saucepot with tall sides, place the brown sugar, baking soda, vanilla, corn syrup, buttermilk, butter, and salt. (This mixture tends to boil over if not watched.) Whisk to combine. Place over medium heat and cook, without stirring, until the sugar starts to bubble, about 3 minutes. Whisk until well combined. Raise the heat to medium-high and bring the sauce to a boil. Reduce the heat to medium-low and simmer, whisking occasionally, until it starts to thicken, about 10 to 15 minutes. Remove from the heat.

▶ Serve the bread pudding warm with the sauce on the side.

Serves 8.

 Cooking Tips: Praline pecans are pecan halves that have been candy-coated. They are sometimes also called candied pecans or bourbon pecans.

Dark brown sugar and dark corn syrup lend a rich molasses flavor to this dessert. It is fine to substitute light brown sugar and light corn syrup if that is what you have on hand.

 Variation: Ideally you should use day-old bread for this dish. It is okay to use fresh bread in a pinch. Day-old brioche or French bread can be substituted for the croissants.

 Do Ahead: The sauce can be stored in the refrigerator for up to 1 week. Reheat in a double boiler or a microwave.

 Time-Saving Tip: It's not as rich in flavor, but you can use store-bought caramel sauce in place of praline sauce.

Rustic Apple Tart

Nothing conjures up Americana more than a slice of apple pie. Don't fuss over having the perfect crust. Instead whip up a rustic version that is meant to look a little rough around the edges. This free-form tart dishes up the sweet apple pie flavor we have all grown to love.

1	unbaked pie crust (9-inch), homemade or store-bought	2	tablespoons all-purpose flour
4	Granny Smith apples (about 1 1/2 pounds), peeled, cored, and cut into thin slices, about 1/4-inch thick	1	teaspoon ground cinnamon
		1/4	teaspoon Kosher salt
1/2	cup plus 2 tablespoons granulated sugar, divided	1	large egg, lightly beaten

▸ Preheat the oven to 375 degrees.

▸ Roll the dough into a 10-inch round, about 1/8-inch thick. Transfer to a rimmed baking sheet lined with parchment paper. Set aside.

▸ In a large mixing bowl combine the apples, 1/2 cup of the sugar, flour, cinnamon, and salt, and toss to coat. Fill the center of the pie crust with the apple mixture in an even layer, leaving a 1 1/2-inch border. Fold the border up and over the apples, overlapping every 2 to 3 inches, to make a rim. Brush the rim with the egg wash, and evenly sprinkle the remaining 2 tablespoons of sugar over the rim.

▸ Bake until the crust is nicely browned and the apples are bubbly, about 30 to 40 minutes. Remove from the oven and let cool on a rack for 15 minutes before serving. Serve warm.

Serves 8.

 Variation: This tart would also be delicious when made with pears.

BASIC
RECIPES

Chicken Stock

Nothing tastes quite like a rich, homemade chicken stock. As you will see from this recipe, the homemade version is simple to make.

1	roasting chicken (3 to 4 pounds)		4	celery ribs, cut into 3- or 4-inch pieces
3	quarts water		1	bay leaf
1	large onion, peeled and cut into eighths		1	teaspoon whole black peppercorns
4	carrots, peeled and cut in half			

▸ Rinse the chicken and trim off all excess fat. Place the chicken in a large soup pot. Add the water. Over high heat, bring to a boil. Using a ladle or large metal spoon, skim off the foam and fat that comes to the surface.

▸ Add the onion, carrots, celery, bay leaf, and peppercorns. Cover, reduce the heat to medium-low, and cook, skimming occasionally, for 2 hours.

▸ Remove the chicken from the pot and reserve it for another use. Discard the onion, carrots, celery, and bay leaf. Strain the stock through a fine-mesh sieve into a large bowl or another large pot.

▸ If using immediately, remove the excess fat by dragging a paper towel over the surface to absorb the fat.

▸ If using later, cool to room temperature and refrigerate. As the liquid cools, the fat will rise to the surface; remove and discard this fat with a large metal spoon before reheating.

Makes about 8 cups.

 Cooking Tips: Don't throw away those chicken bones. It may not be quite as rich as if using raw bones, but you can use the leftover carcass from a roast chicken to make a delicious stock.

The meat from this boiled chicken can be used in any recipe that calls for cooked chicken. (See page xi for a list of ideas.)

 Freezes Well: I like to freeze stock in 1 cup portions so I can thaw just what I need.

Creamy Stone-Ground Grits

Stone-ground grits bear little resemblance to the "quick" grits found in most supermarkets. These golden-yellow grits are coarser in texture and offer a richer corn flavor. Many markets now carry them, but if you can't find them at your local grocery, check at a farmers' market or specialty store. Polenta is an acceptable substitute.

2 cups chicken stock	1 cup stone-ground grits
2 cups milk	Kosher salt and freshly ground black pepper

▸ In a large saucepot combine the chicken stock and milk. Over medium-high heat, bring the mixture to a boil. Whisk in the grits and season with salt and pepper to taste. Reduce the heat to low, cover, and cook, whisking often, until the liquid is absorbed, about 35 to 40 minutes. Adjust seasonings as needed. Serve hot.

Makes 4 cups.

 Cooking Tip: Boiling grits bubble and are very hot. For this reason it is best to use a saucepot with high sides.

 Variation: If you do not have chicken stock, you can substitute water. For an even richer batch of grits, substitute half-and-half or heavy cream for the milk.

Basic Tomato Sauce

This basic tomato sauce is a cinch to make. I usually make a double or triple batch and freeze the extra in 1-cup portions for the next time I need tomato sauce but am short on time.

1 tablespoon olive oil	1 can (28-ounce) crushed tomatoes
1/4 cup finely diced yellow onions	1 teaspoon dried basil
(1/2 small onion)	Kosher salt and freshly ground black pepper
1 clove garlic, minced	

▶ In a medium stockpot over medium-high heat, warm the oil until a few droplets of water sizzle when carefully sprinkled in the pot. Add the onions and garlic, and sauté until soft, about 5 minutes. Add the crushed tomatoes and basil. Season with salt and pepper to taste. Reduce the heat to medium-low and simmer, covered, for 20 to 25 minutes. Adjust the seasonings as needed.

Makes 3 cups.

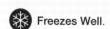 **Freezes Well.**

Pie Crust

This pie crust is light and flaky. Pastry flour offers a more tender crust, but all-purpose flour can be used in a pinch.

1¹/₃ cups pastry or all-purpose flour

¹/₂ teaspoon salt

8 tablespoons (1 stick) cold unsalted butter, cut into ¹/₂-inch cubes

3 to 4 tablespoons ice water

▶ In a food processor, pulse together the flour and salt until combined. Add the butter and pulse until coarse crumbs form, no longer than 25 seconds. Add 3 tablespoons of the water and pulse about 6 times. The dough is ready if it holds together when pinched between your fingers. If it does not hold together, add the remaining tablespoon of water and pulse about 3 times to combine.

▶ Transfer the dough to a clean work surface. Knead once or twice to incorporate any loose bits. Pat into a disk and wrap tightly in plastic wrap. Refrigerate for at least 1 hour before rolling.

Makes one 9-inch pie crust.

 Freezes Well: Tightly sealed dough can be frozen for up to 3 months. Thaw in the refrigerator before using.

Pizza Dough

You will be shocked at how easy it is to make pizza dough with this foolproof food processor recipe. Make sure to use rapid-rise yeast in this recipe. It's much easier than active dry yeast, which has to be activated with hot water before it can be used.

2¹/₂ cups all-purpose flour
1   envelope (¹/₄-ounce) rapid-rise yeast
2   teaspoons Kosher salt
2   tablespoons olive oil, plus extra to brush on the crusts

1   cup cold water
Kosher salt and freshly ground black pepper

▶ In a food processor, pulse together the flour, yeast, and salt. With the processor running, add the oil and then water in a steady stream. Process until the dough just begins to form a ball.

▶ Turn out the dough onto a floured work surface and knead until smooth and elastic, about 4 to 5 times. Place the dough in a resealable plastic bag and let rise at room temperature until it has doubled in size, about 2 hours.

▶ Divide the dough into two equal portions, roll into balls, and cover with a clean kitchen towel or plastic wrap. Let the dough rise until elastic, about 15 to 20 minutes, before shaping, topping, and baking.

▶ Preheat the oven to 500 degrees.

▶ Place each dough ball on a baking sheet. Using your hands, gently flatten, and pull into circles about 10 inches in diameter. Brush each crust with olive oil and season the dough with salt and pepper to taste. Top with your desired pizza toppings. Bake until the crust is golden brown and the toppings are hot, about 10 to 12 minutes.

Makes 2 10-inch pizza crusts or 4 5-inch individual pizzas.

 Do Ahead: You can make dough in the food processor and let it rise overnight in the refrigerator. Just be sure to let it come to room temperature before dividing it and rolling it into balls.

 Freezes Well: Let the dough thaw overnight in the refrigerator before using.

Roasted Red Bell Peppers

You can buy peppers already roasted at the market, but I prefer the less oily texture of a freshly roasted red pepper. Plus it's kinda fun to make!

2   red bell peppers

▶ To roast the red pepper, turn the gas burner, or grill, to high heat. Place the peppers flat on the grate and cook until that side is well charred. Rotate the peppers a quarter turn and repeat until each side is well charred. Place the charred, hot peppers in a resealable bag, seal, and steam until the peppers have cooled to room temperature, about 15 minutes.

▶ Remove the peppers from the bag and, using a paper towel, peel off the skin. Gently pull the peppers apart. Remove and discard all the seeds and the stem. Never rinse the peppers with water, or the flavor will be diminished. Chop or slice the peppers to the desired size.

Makes about 1 cup.

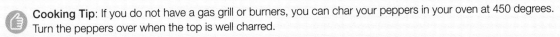 **Cooking Tip**: If you do not have a gas grill or burners, you can char your peppers in your oven at 450 degrees. Turn the peppers over when the top is well charred.

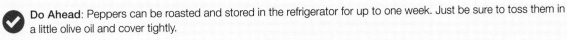 **Do Ahead**: Peppers can be roasted and stored in the refrigerator for up to one week. Just be sure to toss them in a little olive oil and cover tightly.

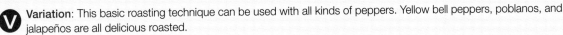 **Variation**: This basic roasting technique can be used with all kinds of peppers. Yellow bell peppers, poblanos, and jalapeños are all delicious roasted.

Many Thanks

My wonderful family, thank you for your love, support, and understanding as I pursue my dreams . . . and play with food! You are the best and make my life complete.

Susan, for generously giving your time and cooking expertise to edit yet another book. I am blessed to have such a wonderful sister!

Allison Lemm and Melissa Petersen, where would I be without such special and talented friends? Thank you for all the time you have spent proofing, lending plates, washing dishes, fluting pie crusts, being my sounding board, and offering words of encouragement.

Mom, for being the grandmother extraordinaire, chauffeuring and babysitting the girls while I worked.

Dad, for sharing your kitchen secrets and your passion for good food.

Maria and Bob, for being wonderful in-laws and helping proofread my book.

Natalie Root, for making this book beautiful with your stunning photography. I want to stick a fork in every page!

Babcock Gifts, Lodge Cast Iron, Maritucker Hanemann, Nancy Kistler, Interim Restaurant, and the Majestic Café, for sharing your picture-perfect pans, dishes, and serving pieces.

To the best group of recipe testers an author could ever ask for: Amy Barry, Susan Barcroft, Cindy Ettingoff, Margaret Fraser, Laura Hanemann, Allison Lemm, Stephanie Linkous, Amy Pearce, Mary Katherine Redd, Macrae Schaffler, Carol Seamons, Will Sharp, Jenny Vergos, and Patricia Wilson.

To the talented cooks who shared secrets from your kitchens: Linda Cornish, Jeff Dunham, Barbara Hanemann, Laura Hanemann, Tom Hanemann, Mia Henley, Lucia Heros, Kristen Keegan, Gay Landaiche, Laurie Major, Emily Martin, Craig Monzio, Melissa Petersen, Heather Bugg Ries, Susan Rogol, Kelly Thompson, Jenny and Nick Vergos, Patricia Wilson, and Linda and Lee Anne Wray.

Amy Barry, Sherri Kimery, and Michelle Wilson, for being the best carpool buddies and driving my girls when I was busy in the kitchen.

Joel Miller, Heather Skelton, Jason Jones, Kristen Vasgaard, and all the folks at Thomas Nelson Publishers who helped bring this book to life.

All my Facebook and Twitter friends (I consider you friends, not fans!), who shared ideas and suggestions to make this book the best it could be.

Credits

Many thanks to Babcock Gifts for the use of their dishes and linens in the following photos:

Lentil and Sausage Soup (page 15)
Chicken Enchiladas with Salsa Verde (page 35)
Chicken Parmesan (page 37)
Shrimp and Grits (page 87)
Pan-Roasted Sea Bass with Chive-Garlic
  Compound Butter (page 85)
Blackened Catfish (page 77)
Shrimp Scampi (page 89)
Lemon Salmon (page 83)
Carnitas (page 59)
Apricot Pork Tenderloin (page 51)
Peppered Filets with a Grainy Mustard Sauce
  (page 69)
Italian Sausage and Spinach Lasagna (page106)
Vongole Clam Sauce (page 115)
Meatball Sub (page 128)

Reuben (page 131)
Grilled Jalapeno Pimento Cheese Sandwich
  (page 127)
Wild Mushroom, Rosemary, and Hazelnut
  Dressing (page 165)
Baked Cheese Grits (page 143)
Sautéed Spaghetti Squash (page 195)
Asparagus with Brown Butter (page 169)
Cheddar-Pecan Green Bean Casserole (page 177)
Lemony Swiss Chard with Pine Nuts and Raisins
  (page 187)
Sautéed Shitake Mushrooms (page 193)
Glazed Carrots (page 183)
Peanut Butter Cup Tart (page 220)

Many thanks to Lodge Cast Iron for the use of their pieces in the following photos:

Potato Chip Chicken Tenders (page 43)
Southwestern Crab Cakes (page 92)
Chicken, Roasted Poblano, and Corn Quesadillas (page 121)
Cornbread and Sausage Stuffing (page 151)

About the Author

When asked why she got into the food business, Jennifer Chandler always quickly responds, "Because I love to eat!"

Jennifer's love of good food has led her down an interesting—and tasty—road over the past 15 years.

In 1993, Jennifer surprised everyone when she told them that she was giving up a career in international finance to move to Paris to learn to cook. Jennifer enrolled at the famed Le Cordon Bleu academy, took a crash course in French and, a year later, graduated at the top of her class with Le Grand Diplome and a Mention Tres Bien in Pastry.

The year she spent in Paris, which included an internship in the pastry shop of Hôtel Plaza Athénée, taught her to appreciate food as something to enjoy and savor.

After that life-changing year in Paris, she cut her teeth in the food biz with a stint at a Washington, D.C. restaurant group, as well as working in the pastry shop at one of the east coast's top caterers.

After moving back home to Memphis, Tennessee, Jennifer briefly considered getting a 9-to-5 career, but soon found herself dreaming of the kitchen.

For several years, Jennifer owned a prepared foods market and bakery in Memphis called Cheffie's Market and More. "Our customers loved the convenience of Cheffie's. They could pick up pre-cooked fresh and delicious meals that only needed to be briefly re-heated to serve," says Chandler. "Our selection of over fifty items—ranging from salads to side-dishes to entrees—was prepared fresh daily by a team of the top chefs in Memphis." Voted "Best New Restaurant in Memphis," Cheffie's received much acclaim and many awards.

With the birth of her second child, though, Jennifer decided to turn her food career into a more family-friendly one and, because she couldn't leave the business altogether, she started food writing.

A contributing writer to several magazines for over 7 years, her first cookbook *Simply Salads: More Than 100 Delicious Creative Recipes made from Prepackaged Greens and a Few Easy-to-Find Ingredients* was released in 2007. In addition to writing, Jennifer has been featured on the Food Network in two episodes of *Dinner Impossible* as well as on Martha Stewart's *Everyday Food* XM/Sirius Radio Program. For more recipes, or to follow Jennifer on Facebook or Twitter, please visit www.cookwithjennifer.com.

About the Photographer

 atalie Root is an alumna of Loyola University–New Orleans, where she earned her BA in communications with an emphasis in photojournalism. A self-proclaimed lover of ham and cheese on white bread, pepperoni pizza, and chicken strips, she has expanded her portfolio as well as her palate via projects with several chefs throughout the Southeast. Her work has been printed in several regional publications. She highly recommends Potato Chip Chicken Tenders and Peppered Filets with Grainy Mustard Cream Sauce—her *Simply Suppers* favorites! Natalie currently resides in New Orleans, where she maintains work as a freelance food photographer.

Index